The Murder of John Francis Dowling and the Massacre of 300 Aborigines

Paul Dillon

Published in 2019 by Connor Court Publishing Pty Ltd

Copyright © Paul Dillon 2019

All rights reserved. No part of this book may be reproduced or transmitted in any form or by any means, electronic or mechanical, including photocopying, recording or by any information storage and retrieval system, without prior permission in writing from the publisher.

Connor Court Publishing Pty Ltd
PO Box 7257
Redland Bay QLD 4165
sales@connorcourt.com
www.connorcourtpublishing.com.au

Phone 0497-900-685

Printed in Australia

ISBN 978-1-925826-50-0

Front Cover Image: ML State Library NSW FL1002478

Contents

About the Author	5
Preface	7
Chapter One - The Deceased	11
Chapter Two - Academic Treatment	23
Chapter Three - The Murder	49
Chapter Four - The Massacre?	61
Summation	81
Epilogue	85
Appendix A - Death Certificate	89
Appendix B - Bulloo River Runs	90
Appendix C - Map of Warrego	91
Appendix D - Dowling Track	93
Appendix E - Letters to the Editor	95
Appendix F - E O Hobkirk Manuscript	105
Appendix G - Relevant Press Reportage relating to John Dowling's Death	115
Appendix H - Colonial Frontier Massacres in Central and Eastern Australia 1788-1930	119
Bibliography	121

About the Author

Paul Dillon is a Townsville based author of *Frederick Walker Commandant of the Native Police*, Connor Court Publishing, Brisbane 2018 and *Red Centre, Dead Centre The True Story of Peter Falconer*, Austin Macauley Publisher, London 2019. He holds a Bachelor of Arts degree from the Australian National University. Paul joined the Commonwealth Public Service in 1965. On 23 May 1986, he was called to the Bar of New South Wales and practised as a barrister in the Criminal Division of the superior courts of Queensland as counsel for the defence.

Preface

I don't suppose this little monograph can escape the tag of being another example of the never-ending debate about the History Wars of Australia. Be that as it may, I am not trying to write about John Dowling's murder by the Blacks from the political dichotomy of the left or the right. I am trying to suggest that there is a lot of woolly thinking out there, as my dear old headteacher used to say, when it comes to the pastoral settlement of Australia and the consequent contact with the Aborigines. There was a time when I thought Universities were centres of excellence, where high-quality research was carried out by intelligent individuals who put intellectual honesty above their greedy little motives to obtain a degree, maxima cum laude. By intellectual honesty I mean:

> An applied method of problem solving, characterized by an unbiased, honest attitude, which can be demonstrated in a number of different ways, including but not limited to: One's personal beliefs do not interfere with the pursuit of truth; Relevant facts and information are not purposefully omitted even when such things may contradict one's hypothesis; Facts are presented in an unbiased manner, and not twisted to give misleading impressions or to support one view over another; References, or earlier work, are acknowledged where possible, and plagiarism is avoided.[1]

---

[1] https://www.definitions.net/definition/Intellectual%20honesty

Alas, I have found that I am deluded. We live in a world where honesty and truth take a back seat, when it comes to the social justice agenda. The world can no longer can handle the truth. The social justice warrior and his rag-tag, social media mob have taken over and they have infiltrated all walks of life where the ends justify the means. So, if you achieve your goal of knocking over the white Anglo bogeyman and also get a doctorate on the way then, hey, you've earned a bonus.

I know universities no longer exclude people as they once did like Jews, Catholics, Quakers, women, the poor, coloureds and other undesirable types but now run sheltered workshops where the anomie are made whole again, so they can live a full and fruitful campus life and perhaps, even be allowed to walk on the quadrangle lawn. But are the undergraduates and sundry other trolls who loiter about the temple of Athena tutored in the traditional skills of historical methodology? Such as source criticism: the process of evaluating the qualities of an information source, its validity, reliability, and relevance to the subject under investigation.

> When was the source, written or unwritten, produced (date)?
> Where was it produced (localization)?
> By whom was it produced (authorship)?
> From what pre-existing material was it produced (analysis)?
> In what original form was it produced (integrity)?
> What is the evidential value of its contents (credibility)?[2]

---

[2] Gilbert J Garraghan and Jean Delanglez divide source criticism into six inquiries. https://en.wikipedia.org/wiki/Historical_method

Of course, the researcher cannot ignore Bill Stanner's injunction that the Aborigines have been left out of Australian history and they must now be given a voice. How to achieve this is easier said than done and most historians take the easy way out either through sloth or ignorance and simply assume the role of the Aborigines' advocate totally ignoring the conflict of interest that arises when a professional historian is engaged in putting forward a dissertation on a particular topic or event where impartiality and accuracy are imperatives.

So Australian history has wandered off into the dreamtime of *Bury My Heart at Wounded Knee*, rather than sticking to the good ole days of camping by a billabong, stuffing a jumbuck in your tucker bag, building grass castles, yarn telling and singing, *don't bury me on the lone prairie*. The myths of Henry Lawson are gone forever. The drover's wife, instead of leaving a saucer of milk out for the snake so the dog can kill it, now sits at Hornet Bank or Cullin la Ringo daydreaming:

> He lifted his head from his drinking, as cattle do,
> And looked at me vaguely, as drinking cattle do,
> I picked up a clumsy log
> And threw it at the water-trough with a clatter.
> I think it did not hit him,
> But suddenly that part of him that was left behind convulsed in undignified haste.
> Writhed like lightning, and was gone.[3]

---

[3] DH Lawrence, *The Snake*.

But she knows that tomorrow he will come, spear and tomahawk in hand. They will find her, legs akimbo with her sweet and gentle countenance cleft asunder, while her brains will lay in vivid disarray upon this sacred soil because she had invaded the rainbow serpent's bower of lovely springs, babbling brooks and eucalypts blossoms.

The second injunction may be found in the works of Henry Reynolds where he says, "… reading mainly European texts against the grain, as it is often called, it was possible to create a picture of an indigenous response".[4] What this actually means is not clear to me and how you apply this technique is equally unclear. But I am reminded of Alice when she said: "But 'glory' doesn't mean 'a nice knock-down argument'." "When I use a word," Humpty Dumpty said, in rather a scornful tone, "it means just what I choose it to mean—neither more nor less."[5]

---

[4] Reynolds, Henry *The Other Side of the Frontier* UNSW Press 2006 p 4.
[5] Carroll, L *Through the Looking-Glass* Raleigh, NC: Hayes Barton Press, 1872, p. 72.

1

The Deceased

The following Death Notice appeared in the *Sydney Morning Herald* of 9 September 1865:

> On or about the 12th June last (murdered when asleep by the Blacks), while on his way from the Paroo River to Mount Murchison, John Francis, youngest son of the late Willoughby James Dowling, Esq., of Bathurst.[6]

John Francis Dowling's Death Certificate states, he died on 13 June 1865 on the Paroo River, Queensland having been murdered by the Blacks and was buried in the Randwick Cemetery on 27 October 1866. Who was John Francis Dowling? He was the youngest son of Willoughby James Dowling (1812-1849), of Bathurst, who was the nephew and associate of Sir

---

[6] See also *Empire* 11 September 1865, p. 1, *Sydney Mail*, 16 September 1865, p. 9, *Sydney Morning Herald*, 21 September, 1865, p 11.

James Dowling (1787 – 1844), Chief Justice of the Supreme Court of New South Wales. Willoughby Dowling had come to Australia with his uncle, Sir James, as the judge's associate. John Francis was also the younger brother of Vincent James Dowling (1835-1903). Vincent James is renowned in Australian pastoral history as a very successful explorer and pastoral entrepreneur as the following briefly shows:

> Mr Dowling established the Fort Bourke[7] station on the Darling. At the time, there was only one station, Gundabooka, occupied in that part of the colony. Finding the country becoming 'too civilized' on the Darling, Mr Dowling commenced exploring, and discovered the Paroo, Bulloo, and other good country in Queensland. He formed stations upon the Warrego, Cuttaburra, and spring country at Yantabulla, and also formed Caiwarroo and Eulo, on the Paroo. He entered into partnership with Mr GH Cox, and formed stations on the Paroo and Thargomindah, also a large cattle station on the Bulloo, at which place he settled down, and lived for many years, selling out eventually in 1875. As a pioneer of new country, Mr Dowling had a very rough time with both blacks and whites.[8]

John Dowling it seems had worked for his older brother Vincent, possibly as a superintendent on one of Vincent's stations.[9] Mr Arthur Bloxam, of Tooralle, River Darling gave

---
[7] Bourke NSW 2840
[8] *Sydney Mail and New South Wales Advertiser* 29 November 1884 p. 1087.
[9] Orders Drawn by Messrs Cox and Dowling, or John Dowling on Messrs Lamb, Parbury, and Co., will be duly paid on presentation at the Commercial Bank. The Commercial Banking Company will also pay orders drawn by R K Sams or A Laws, on the undersigned. J de V Lamb Sydney, 2nd March, 1865. SMH 4 March 1865 p 7.

the following account of the Bulloo area:

22 October 1864, ... The Bulloo Valley here is from 15 to 20 miles wide, well grassed, and abundantly watered, and bounded on either side by mulga-timbered sandstone ridges or hills of considerable elevation, the slopes of which are pretty and of good stock-carrying capacity. The country just here I found to have been settled on by two cattle-holders, of the names of Dowling and Sams, from the upper Paroo country, for about a month. They told me they got a capitally watered road out directly east of them from that river. They are in latitude 28° S, and in longitude 143° 20 E, the nearest point of Cooper's Creek, as laid down by Gregory, being 80 miles west-south-west of their camp; and Eulo, Mr Dowling's station on the Paroo, being 82 miles east. Fort Bourke, on the Darling, lies 300 miles south-east and by south from them. A point, half-way between Mount Murchison and Mr M'Pherson's on the Darling, 220 miles south by east; to Menindee, Darling River, 231 miles south-west by south; to Sydney, south-east, half-east-south-east, 735 miles; to Melbourne, south and by east, 840 miles; to Brisbane, east by north, 700 miles. After spending a day or two at Mr Dowling's and Mr Sams' camp to refresh the horses a little and to gather as much information about the country as possible from the blacks, who muster very strong on these waters, I proceeded down the valley in south-west and west-south-west directions for about ninety miles, running the Bulloo waters out into an immense polygonum swampy system with lakes in it of considerable size, thickly peopled by blacks, who designate the swamp system as "Cary a pundy," having separate names for the lakes and numerous creeks which

flow from the northward into it. I found the Bulloo Valley to maintain its capable stock-carrying qualities and well-watered character the whole way down to this point, where I think the 29th parallel crosses the Grey Ranges, the east side of which hems in this swamp system, which is just within the New South Wales territory ...[10]

The Mount Murchison Station referred to above is that place situated at 31° 26' 52.19" S, 143° 39' 34.09" E now known as Wilcannia, NSW. It was a trading centre for northern cattle into the Victorian gold boom market; fat cattle selling on the Warrego at £6 10s. at yard, were met by Melbourne dealers at Mount Murchison, and bought on the advanced figure of £8.[11]

One of the local papers noted:

> That this District of the Warrego is of greater extent than Great Britain itself, about 660 miles distant from the seat of Government, and of which one of the Government confessed, in June (1864), that they knew nothing except that they received the License Fees for Runs. That this District has received no protection from the hostile natives—with which it swarms—except a small force of Native Police, under Lieutenant Lambert, who, although a very meritorious officer, finds it impossible with his force to guard efficiently a district extending in length to 600 miles. The district also abounds with bushrangers and cattle-stealers.[12]

---

[10] *Sydney Morning Herald*, 8 May 1865, p. 5. He gives Dowling's location as latitude 28°S, and in longitude 143°20 E, putting his station very near the modern town of Thargomindah.
[11] *Brisbane Courier*, 15 September 1866, p. 6.
[12] *Rockhampton Bulletin and Central Queensland*, 21 March 1865 p. 3.

Vincent Dowling had twelve blocks on the Paroo River[13] with a frontage to the river of 120 miles with an area approximately covering 300 square miles. The Caiwarroo homestead was at the lower reaches of the Paroo and consisted of a cottage, stockyards, and woolshed, while Eulo was at the northern end of the runs with a good stockman's hut and yards. The economy of the Warrego appeared to operate as follows, with the trade of the Upper Warrego proceeding towards Rockhampton, while the Lower Warrego and westward of that received their supplies at Fort Bourke, where they were brought by steamers from Echuca, Victoria and Goolwa, South Australia; the rate of carriage of wool from Fort Bourke to Melbourne or Adelaide was at the rate of £12 per ton. The navigation of these rivers by Captain Cadell had done much to open up the interior of Western Queensland.[14] Vincent Dowling's properties were situated geographically thus, starting from Cunnamulla, Eulo was about thirty miles west on the Paroo and Ciawarroo was about forty miles south of Eulo, also on the Paroo. It seems the indigenous people of the Paroo are called the Budjiti People in Queensland[15] and the Bulloo River mob are called the Kullilli. In regards the Bulloo River, the Commissioner of Crown Lands, Barron had measured some 200 miles of the Bulloo frontage, whereon

---

[13] Caiwarro Right, Caiwarro Left, Kyering Right, Kyering Left, Podmore Right, Podmore Left, Thurnby, Flinton, Eulo Right, Eulo Left, Lower Eulo Right, Lower Eulo Left. *Sydney Morning Herald*, 7 July 1868, p. 7.
[14] *Queensland Times, Ipswich Herald and General Advertiser*, 28 January 1864, p. 3.
[15] QCD2015/007 - Budjiti People - Native Title Determination Details.

he located the several holdings known as Bulloo Downs, Cheshunt, Thargomindah (Thuringowa), Norley, Ardock[16], and Comongin. For the uninitiated, Mount Murchison Station is almost due south of Caiwarroo, 28° 38' 39.88" S and as the crow flies, the distance would be approximately 194 miles or 310 kilometres. The Paroo Catchment has a semi-arid to arid climate and is an area of low rainfall and high evaporation with an annual average rainfall in the range of 200 to 400 millimetres with almost 70% of the area receiving on average less than 300 millimetres per annum (DNR 2000).

The Warrego pastoral economy meant a lot to Vincent Dowling, having invested heavily in grazing land, station plant and livestock, with Fort Bourke being an important trading outlet to the lucrative Victoria gold boom market for his livestock. As one of the leading investors in the district, he was sensitive to factors that adversely impacted on his assets and the market he hoped to exploit. The following letter to the Editor of the *Sydney Morning Herald* gives a good picture of Dowling's make-up:

> In your issue of the 10th ultimo, I notice an extract from the *Darling Downs Gazette*, giving an account, in a very precise manner, of my unpleasant murder by the blacks on the river Paroo. As I have been reported killed by the blacks in so many different papers, perhaps you will be good enough, in your widely spread journal, to contradict the report. I am not defunct, neither has there been the slightest foundation or groundwork for such a

---

[16] The correct spelling is Ardoch. It was a station formed out of Owthorpe Runs 3, 4, 5, 8, 9 & 10 by A B Buchanan, MLA, circa 1870, see Appendix B.

report obtaining currency. The blacks on the Paroo, are about the most useful and certainly the quietest I have ever known in any part of the colony. I believe this cruel report was circulated by a gentleman who has a station about twenty miles from our lower cattle station, on the Paroo. So impressed was this gentleman with the murder of myself or brother, that he never sent to inquire or see if assistance was required. There is very little faith to be placed in the reports relative to murders by the blacks in this part of the colony, as white men coming in from the back stations, circulate such reports in order to deter their fellows from venturing back; by this means the scoundrels try to keep up a high rate of wages.

To give you an idea of what men will say and report in this district in reference to the blacks, I may mention the following: An overseer of my own, on his way out to the Paroo, met a man who informed him that Mr John Dowling (my brother), had been killed by the blacks. The overseer said he did not believe him, when the man replied he might with safety do so, as he was one of the identical men who buried him. By inserting the above, you will much oblige. Yours truly, Vincent Dowling. Warpuelar, Fort Bourke, 1st May 1864.[17]

Vincent could do little about the weather or the environment in which his grazing empire was located, which he talked up at all times, but in regards outside influences like the press he was sensitive to criticism and protective of his industry. So, when the local press in the form of the Bourke correspondent for the *Maitland Mercury and Hunter River General Advertiser* began to

---

[17] *Sydney Morning Herald*, 11 July 1864, p. 3.

write highly lurid copy about life in Bourke and the surrounding district, Vincent saw the press comment as scurrilous, yellow journalism designed to damage his empire in a number of ways, particularly making the place appear unattractive to investors, labourers, shearers, merchants and trades people and with the further consequence of driving up wages and thus increasing his cost of production with the possible consequences of reduced margins leading to an unviable enterprise. In response to the Bourke correspondent and the *Maitland Mercury*, he placed an advertisement in the *Herald* condemning both and restating his views that the Warrego and in particular the Blacks, were all happiness and light. Perhaps there was a further dimension to the issue, after all Vincent had been appointed a magistrate of the district and the law and order issue may have been something he took personally.[18] Moreover, in early 1862 Vincent had been appointed a magistrate in Queensland.[19] The advertisement produced a backlash from interested whites and some responded by describing the Blacks as treacherous and the country, a dangerous place to be:

> … Men have been attacked and killed by the blacks, Mr Dowling himself among the former. Men have perished for want of water: N.B., James Dwyer (one of Mr Dowling's men), Kelly, Mason, Richards, and Mr Sullivan's stockman; another is missing; seven or eight men have been picked up in a dying state. And your correspondent did his duty in warning travellers against coming into this waterless

---

[18] *Sydney Mail*, 1 December 1860, p. 4.
[19] *Courier*, 30 January 1862, p. 2.

country. This is a perfect desert.[20]

It was in these circumstances that John Dowling in the early part of June 1865 left his home on the Paroo River, in the company of "Waddy Galo" a blackfellow belonging to the Buela River,[21] with the intention of cutting a road from the Paroo to Mount Murchison. The initial public report of John Dowling's death is as follows:

> We have received from a correspondent the following account of the murder of Mr John Dowling, briefly mentioned in our last. The communication is undated, and the postmark (Bourke) is in this respect illegible: I have this week a most mournful task to fulfil—one of those fearful events which every now and then places the district in which it occurs in profound gloom and sorrow from eight or ten weeks ago Mr John Dowling (brother of Mr Vincent Dowling) left his home on the Paroo River, in company of a "Waddy Galo" blackfellow belonging to the Buela River, with the intention of cutting a road from the Paroo to Mount Murchison. Time passed away, and no news came in from the lonely pioneer; no one had seen him or knew of his whereabout. After six weeks of uncertainty, Mr William Hall, with Mr George Podmore, accompanied by a black, started on the tracks of the absent one. On through the silent solitude rode the two friends, passing the camping places which had been weeks before occupied by the object of their search, full of doubt and foreboding.

---

[20] The Reader is asked to review the material at Appendix E hereto.
[21] This appears to be a misspelling of Bulloo.

They travel on the trail with the unerringness of a sleuth hound; they enter a waterless tract, and after passing thirty or forty miles, their journey is brought to a painful close. Beside the scattered embers of a small fire, in the awful stillness of the desert, lay the earthly remains of the murdered settler; beside him and around lay the various articles belonging to the deceased—there were his rations, blankets, saddles, undischarged pistols; and from a diary found on the scene of murder, picked and tossed about by the crows, was read the last entry of the unfortunate young man. Only four entries had been made since he departed from his home, and these of trifling importance. The last one states that the blacks could tell him "no more about the springs." He was evidently at fault as to his position. They had travelled a long way without water, and still were distant from it many miles. From the last entry made, the writer had perished just seven weeks, and nothing was remaining by which he could be recognised save his hair and clothes. One blow seems to have been given, which crashed in the skull. No articles were removed from the dead, not even the rations. All remained as the too confident explorer had left them on the night of his violent death—his murderer evidently flying from the scene as soon as his diabolical deed was accomplished. With sorrowful hearts Messrs Hall and Podmore gathered up the wreck of their lost friend, and hurried with their mournful burden upon their back track. Mr John Dowling was a young man of great bush experience, a kind friend, and an indulgent master. His untimely death has caused deep sorrow in all who knew him. I have since heard that the murder was committed early in the evening, as a pile of wood collected for the night lay unburnt; also, that a large stick was found, bloody, and with portion of the deceased's hair sticking to it. Probably sleep came across the traveller soon after camping, which proved to be the sleep of death.[22]

The Sydney papers, the *Empire* and the *Sydney Morning Herald* also ran the story but included some interesting additional facts:

> ... in the early part of June last Mr John Dowling left one of Cox and Dowling's stations, near the border with one blackfellow, who was supposed to know the country; the last entry being the 13th of June. The horses have not yet been found.[23] ... has been murdered by the blacks, near Bourke.[24]

The *Brisbane Courier* in running with the story of John Dowling's murder thought the case worthy of their considered opinion:

> The further particulars, moreover, which we have of the murder of Mr Dowling, on the Darling, do not supply much food for congratulation to the "Aborigines' Friends Society." The body was found, with the skull fractured, and the piece of wood which had affected the murder lying by, all bloody. I must confess that I am somewhat puzzled about this murder. The first account was that Mr Dowling was accompanied only by one black guide; and if this were so, I believe bushmen will agree with me that a murder under these circumstances was an unusual

---

[22] *Maitland Mercury and Hunter River General Advertiser*, 31 August 1865, p. 2; *Sydney Mail*. 2 September 1865, p. 4.
[23] *Empire*, 29 August 1865, p. 4.
[24] *Sydney Morning Herald*, 21 September 1865, p. 5.

thing. If they were afterwards joined by other blacks, of course the case is different. Mr Dowling appears to have lain down, no doubt fatigued with the day's journey, and to have fallen asleep where he was murdered. The wood had been gathered together for making the fire, had it had not been lighted. Mr Dowling's rations, arms, and clothing were lying about untouched. Altogether it is a strange affair. Mark my words, the protectionist will find an apology. Mr Dowling was in search of water, and an entry found in his journal, wherein he says that the blacks refused to show him the springs, will be taken as conclusive evidence that they killed him in order to preserve the small supply of water necessary for the existence of the tribe. And, between you and I, I don't think that this opinion would be far astray after all.[25]

The above newspaper reportage represents the only statements recorded contemporaneously with the death of John Francis Dowling. It appears that no inquest was conducted into his death as no record of it has been found to date. His death certificate was issued by the colony of Queensland and records his death as murdered by the Blacks on the Paroo River, Queensland. Death in the Australian outback was not uncommon in the nineteenth century by many and various means or causes. Many Australians, black or white remain even to this day where they fell, unburied and unmourned. However, John Dowling was a member of a family that had money, status and clout. He wasn't a swaggie humpin his bluey on the wallaby track never to be seen or heard of again.

---

[25] *Brisbane Courier*, 5 September 1865, p. 3.

2

Academic Treatment

Writing in 1888, Charles F Maxwell observed that Vincent Dowling:

> Although exposed to frequent attacks from the blacks, he escaped without hurt, but not without some close shaves, as on one occasion he had a spear driven through his hat; and on another a boomerang thrown by a wild man cut open the ribs of the mare he was riding. Yet he did not retaliate, and not until 1865, when his brother John was murdered by the blacks, did he ever shed a drop of blackfellow's blood.[26]

It is regrettable that Mr Maxwell, who no doubt was an honourable gentleman, should be responsible for putting bad thoughts and mis-information into the minds of the digital knights-errant of today, who tilt at the windmills of Australian colonial history with the deluded belief they are righting

---

[26] Maxwell, Charles F., *Australian Men of Mark 1788 – 1888*, Sydney 1888, Volume 1, p. 385.

the wrongs of yesteryear. The above statement by Maxwell is wrong and without foundation of any kind. I quote from Vincent James Dowling's diary:

> 22 June 1863. While off my horse examining fresh black tracks to ascertain their age while stooping was rather surprised at getting a spear through my hat from the opposite side of the creek carried off and pinned it to the ground, no time for reflection before I was saluted with four boomerangs, none of which took effect but the last which struck the saddle and horse, tearing off flap of the saddle cut it almost like a knife. Picked up the boomerangs 3 and spear with my hat on the top of it cantered out of shot. I had a narrow escape four inches lower and the spear a fine barbed one would have pierced my left temple. I shall always wear long American hats. The Blacks must have taken me to be long headed which I am not by the bye and thus my hat saved me. Must never leave camp without arms again. After recovering from my surprise went out back and up the creek a little struck in and found good water holes. Returned down the creek keeping away from the banks. I stopped for an hour 3 miles up from where I struck the creek, fed my horse, bridle in hand, too close to the darkies. Rounded up three blacks on returning home and found the name of the creek to be the Coocara. Had some difficulty in stopping these gentlemen. They would not stop until I touched up one with the point of my spear. ... Got back to camp at Sundown and found old Tom all right, poor fellow. I am glad I escaped for his sake, he would have been in a terrific fix. I need not say how thankful I feel to

Providence for my escape. Death is often closer to us than we think.

29 June ... Drove on down the creek (Cutha Paroo) met an old blackfellow and his gin in about 7 miles, they invited me to spend the evening with them. I accepted their invitation, they made me a fire and picked some grass for my bed, were exceedingly attentive and polite, on the whole spent rather an agreeable evening. How little satisfies one, if one could only believe in it. Ingenuas dedicisse fidelibus notes et cet. [I think Vincent means: The note of love is gentle and ardent; that of anger, loud and turbulent.]

30 June. Started my hostess Kitty, I find is her name, for the horses at daybreak. She brought them up and acknowledged her reward in the shape of half a fig of tobacco. Ascertained in the course of conversations these are Cooinoo last night (and) that there is a spring near Birrewarra right bank and that there are several between the Paroo and Cutha Paroo. Bid adieu to my hosts very early having given them a pressing invitation to visit the sheep station on the Irara which they have excepted (sic).[27]

In late December 1922, EO Hobkirk handed to William Gall, Under Secretary in the Home Secretary's Department, Brisbane two manuscripts seeking to sell them for 10/-. Gall described Hobkirk to the anonymous buyer as "an old identity of South West of Queensland." The relevant manuscript is called, *The Murder of Mr John Dowling. Locality, Bulloo River*

---

[27] ML MSS 2241/2 item 4.

Queensland and is a hand-written document of approximately 1700 words in length written in 1922 about an event that "happened in 1865, 57 years ago." The full article may be seen at Appendix F. The structure of the document is in the form of a narrative commencing with a statement of principle that Aborigines prefer death before disloyalty. They never betray their own tribesmen. Hobkirk then describes the lead up to the disappearance of John Dowling, the search for him, the finding of his remains and then the investigation of his death culminating in the massacre of the Bulloo Aborigines because of their dumb insolence towards a white man seeking answers to a white man's problem. During the course of the telling, Hobkirk confesses to being a party to the killing of the Aborigines but only under the orders of a superior and that he did not actually kill any Aborigines. Being an eye witness to the slaughter of the Aborigines for their principle of steadfastness and staunchness, he effectively kills two birds with the one stone. He proves his observation that loyalty to one's tribe is paramount to Aborigines and he has also witnessed a leading squatter, a pillar of society, a Magistrate, dirty his hands with criminal acts thus portraying his rank hypocrisy. The second part of the story is how Hobkirk solved the murder of John Dowling, captured the culprit Pimpilly and turned him reluctantly over to Vincent Dowling's overseer and was never heard of again. The story ends with Hobkirk not receiving any acknowledgment or reward for services rendered to Vincent

Dowling. The question is, firstly, is this document a valid historical source and if so, what weight should be given to the version of events set out in the document?

Also attached to the above Gall note was a second handwritten manuscript titled, *Impersonating an Aboriginal*. This is a story of Hobkirk in 1867, disguising himself as an Aborigine and joining-in a corrobboree:

> We blackened with charcoal a thin, white singlet and a pair of underpants and then painted the front of the singlet with red and white stripes. The blacks paint their skin with red and white ochre, also a pair of black stockings, which we had managed to get possession of; my headgear consisted of a wig, made of horsehair, decorated with emu and white cockatoo parrot feathers. This completed the makeup.

This article appeared in the *Queenslander* of 12 May 1923. The article about the murder of John Dowling did not appear in the press but formed a small part of an article called *Aboriginal Characteristics* published by the *Daily Mail* of 6 January 1923 as follows:

> Another strange characteristic is that natives seldom will betray their own race. Mr John Dowling was cruelly murdered by his pet black boy in the Bulloo River district when camped, out together, but this was not proved until many months after. Although the whole, or many of the tribe knew all about it, they would not betray the murderer, so in consequence, sacrificed their own lives.

Might an inference be drawn from the fact that since the above articles were written for publication in the popular press and as a consequence were never held out by either the publishers or the author as statements of fact as one might find in affidavits or other document of that nature or in scholarly works of history or science, that the articles were written only for the purposes of leisure, entertainment and recreation?

The next version is given by J St. Pierie who in 1969 compiled *Some Information on the History of South-West Queensland*:

> Vincent Dowling was killed by the natives while mustering stock in sandhill country on what is now Wongetta Station, and was buried near the old Thargomindah crossing near Thargomindah homestead. As a reprisal, troopers who found the tribe camped on the eastern side of the river about thirty miles downstream (near the present Thyangra homestead), chased them towards the hills shooting them down as they ran. Until ten or twelve years ago it was not unusual to come across aboriginal skulls in that area. Reports are that the whole tribe of nearly 300 was wiped out. In 1911 there was an old aborigine at Norely who claimed to be the sole survivor of the massacre. A piccaninny at the time, his mother had hidden him under bark in a hole in the floor of the gunyah. The troopers had burnt the camp, including the gunyahs, over his head, but he stayed there and crawled out later. (Information from Mr G Gooch

who went to Norley as a book-keeper in 1911). Date of the massacre is uncertain but it was probably 1872 or earlier as in 1872 Frederick W Armytage bought Thargomindah and Norely stations paying £170,000 for the former and £110,000 for the latter.[28]

Now this version is even more outrages than Hobkirk's. It does not even refer to John Dowling but Vincent, who died peacefully in his bed at Rylstone, NSW in 1903.[29] Let us be generous and say it's a typographical error, and instead of 'Vincent' it should read 'John'. It still makes no sense. When St. Pierie is compared and contrasted with Hobkirk and the 1865 press reportages, the inconsistency and disparity are beyond question and reconciliation. Moreover, the 1865 press reports completely destroy the credibility of the Hobkirk and the Gooch/St. Pierie versions making them unreliable and discredited sources.

---

[28] Warrego and South West Queensland Historical Society, *A collection of papers on the history and other subjects to relating to Cunnamulla and district / prepared by members [of] the Warrego and South West Queensland* Historical Society. Cunnamulla: The Society; 1969, Vol 1, ch 18, p. 3.

[29] *Sydney Morning Herald*, 6 November 1903, p. 4.

The Murder of John Francis Dowling

Incident	1865 Version	1922 Hobkirk	1969 J St. Pierie
Deceased	John Dowling	John Dowling	Vincent Dowling
Departure Point	Caiwarroo Paroo	Thouringowa Bulloo	N/A
Guide	Waddy Galo	Pimpilly	N/A
Reason for travel	Cutting a road	Exploration	Mustering
Destination	Mount Murchison	Menindee	N/A
Duration of travel	Four full days	Not clear/not stated	N/A
Search party	Podmore & Hall	Sams & stockman	N/A
Duration of search	Travelled 30 or 40 miles from Paroo	2 days 60 miles from Cheshunt Bulloo	N/A
Place of Death	Paroo River Queensland	Bulloo River Queensland	Wongatta Station
Date of Death	13 June 1865	Not clear/not stated	1872
Environment	Waterless track of country, lost	Good country couldn't locate water	Sandhill country
Manner of death	Single blow to head, crushing skull	Blow to head, struggle then several blows to skull	Not stated
Reason for death	unknown	To avoid further beatings	Not stated
Crime scene	Camp site undisturbed	Camp site looted	Not stated
Perpetrator	unknown	Pimpilly	Tribe of Blacks
Horses	Not found	Nearby mudfat plenty of water good feed	Not stated

Perhaps the first post-November eleven 1975 crusader to deal with John Dowling's death was Bobbie Hardy in his book *Lament of the Barkindji*:

> When John Dowling's body was found some weeks after his murder on the Paroo in 1865, nothing in the camp has been touched, neither rations, blankets, saddles, pistols nor the dead man's clothing. The assailant was thought to be a Wadikali tribesman, far from his home on the Bulloo, who was helping Dowling survey a track from Mount Murchison to the Paroo. Why he felt impelled to crash his waddy down on his skull was a mystery, but not one that Dowling's friends deemed worthy of much pondering. The fundamental fact was that another white man had been killed by "the niggers", and it behoved his compatriots to take their revenge.[30]

For this event, Hardy cited the *Sydney Mail*, 2 September 1865. Hardy's treatment of the facts seems fair but his comments are emotive and inflammatory. There is no proof that any white man took revenge against the Wadikali tribe or any other tribe over John Dowling's death.

The next to deal with the matter was Hazel McKellar, in *Matyu-mundu* where she recounts the Gooch/St. Pierie version:

> As with other groups, the Kullilla suffered at the hands of the whitefella's rifle. The most notable massacre occurred around 1872. Vincent Dowling, the owner of

---

[30] Hardy, Bobbie, *Lament for the Barkindji: the vanished tribes of the Darling River region*, Rigby, Adelaide, 1976, p. 116.

> Thargomindah station, was killed, according to white history, by aborigines while mustering stock in sandhill country. As a reprisal, troopers found the tribe camped on the eastern side of the river, chased them towards the hills, shooting them down as they ran. It was reported that nearly 300 people were killed in this incident. Some whites say these people belonged to the "Bitharra" tribe but Peter Hood, a Kullilla descendant, is certain they were his people. He says the site of this massacre was further south towards Bulloo Downs.[31]

However, she does not acknowledge Gooch/St. Pierie as the source; there are no citations. McKellar does not attempt a critical analysis of the source material. She makes no comment about the identity of the deceased. Is it Vincent Dowling or John Dowling, or just another white man? Suggesting, it may be irrelevant since it is white history. She says the white history is wrong as to the tribe massacred, as it was the Kullilla and not the Bitharra and the nominated site of the massacre was further south of Bulloo Downs on the authority of Peter Hood, a Kullilla descendant. This perhaps suggests that white history is irrelevant but where it corroborates a tribal story (oral history) then it derives some historical value to koori culture but apart from that it is meaningless white man's business. The issue for McKellar is that Kullilla tribes' people were killed without excuse or justification on the Bulloo River south of Bulloo Downs by troopers in 1872 and not by the

---

[31] McKellar, Hazel *Matya-mundu: a history of the Aboriginal people of South West Queensland* edited by Thom Blake, Cunnamulla Australian Native Welfare Association 1984 p 57.

Dowling family or their agents or servants.³² Where books in the McKellar genre sit in the world of scholarly research, I cannot say, but I imagine there is a place for them in the social justice library.

Perhaps the next attempt at dealing with the John Francis Dowling incident is by Jonathon Richards who completed a Doctor of Philosophy thesis called, *A Question of Necessity: The Native Police in Queensland*, Griffith University, March 2005. I quote from Richards's thesis:

> One credible account of a killing perpetrated by squatters and their employees, is found in the reminiscences of Edward Hobkirk, an employee at Dowling's Station on the Bulloo River.¹⁰⁷ According to Hobkirk, grazier John ('Jack') Dowling was killed in 1864 by his 'pet blackboy' and Dowling's brother wrote to the nearest Native Police (probably Bungil Creek near Roma) about the murder. Hobkirk said Dowling was told to 'take what measures he thought best to revenge the murder,' so 'all the men in the neighbourhood' were assembled and 'armed with revolvers and rifles' before the local Aboriginal people were mustered.¹⁰⁸ Hobkirk admitted he helped bury the bodies that Dowling and others shot at several camps.¹⁰⁹
>
> ¹⁰⁷ EO Hobkirk, *Original Reminiscences of South West Queensland*, NLA, MS 3460, Vol 2. It is unclear when Hobkirk actually wrote this account, but the other records in the file cover the period from 1870 to 1923. Hobkirk gave his manuscript to William Gall at the Home Secretary's Office in 1922.
>
> ¹⁰⁸ Hobkirk, *Original Reminiscences*. The Dowling brothers were

---

³² McKellar, 1984 p 57.

the nephews of Sir James Dowling, A New South Wales judge, and related to other leading squatter families. See a family tree of the Dowling family in David Denholm, *The Colonial Australians* (Melbourne: Penguin, 1979), 177, and a list of their relatives (including James Morisset) in Anthony Dowling (editor), *Reminiscences of a Colonial Judge: James Sheen Dowling* (Sydney: The Federation Press, 1996), 202. John Dowling's death was confirmed in the *Brisbane Courier* (4 June 1864), and the repercussions are mentioned in Bobbie Hardy, *Lament for the Barkindji: the vanished tribes of the Darling River region* (Adelaide: Rigby, 1976), 116.

[109] One source says Vincent Dowling 'subsequently became a terror to the black' Charles F Maxwell, *Australian men of Mark 1788 – 1888* 1 (Sydney: Charles F Maxwell, no date), 385.[33]

Richards relies entirely on Hobkirk for his description of the John Dowling incident. He describes Hobkirk as a credible witness. Richards says, Hobkirk says John Dowling was killed in 1864 and that Hobkirk was "an employee at Dowling's Station on the Bulloo River". Hobkirk in fact says 1865 and clearly states, "... Mr Sams of Cheshunt cattle station, where I was employed." Richards further quotes Hobkirk, "helped bury the bodies;" Hobkirk in fact said, "I helped first to burn the bodies and then to bury them." These errors and omissions are critical and reflect a lack of attention to detail when accuracy is critically required. In footnote 108, Richards says "John Dowling's death was confirmed in the *Brisbane Courier* (4 June 1864)." This statement is blatantly wrong. If Richards had searched the Queensland Register of Deaths, he would have found that John Dowling died on 13 June 1865 on the Paroo River, Queensland. Moreover, if he had checked

---

[33] Richards, Thesis pp 242-243.

Bobbie Hardy's footnote at page 116 of Hardy's above book, Richards would have been referred to an article at page 2 of the *Sydney Mail* of 2 September 1865 which he would have then found a version totally different to Hobkirk's account. In other words, he would have been duty bound to explore and bring to light what the newspapers of the day had to say. This he failed to do. There is no scholarly analysis of the incident.

The next text to deal with the death of John Dowling is *One Hour More Daylight* by Mark Copland, Jonathan Richards and Andrew Walker first published in 2006 but republished in 2010, at page 78 it reads:[34]

> A chilling account of the killing of Aboriginal people in the far southwest can be found in the reminiscences of E. O. Hobkirk, a man described as "an old identity of South Western Queensland." In 1861 Vincent Dowling 'took up' stations on the Paroo River; an attack in 1863 was supposed to have been averted by his 'long American hat', which deflected a spear.[228] In 1865 his brother John Dowling, manager of 'Thouringowa' station on the Bulloo River, was reported as having been killed by his 'pet black boy'. Vincent Dowling gathered the white men in the neighbourhood and started on a search for the alleged culprit 'Pimpilly'. Hobkirk described Dowling's revenge:
>
>> Mr V Dowling, who could talk the blacks' lingo pretty well asked several of them 'who killed white

---

[34] *One hour more daylight: a historical overview of Aboriginal dispossession in southern and southwest Queensland* Mark Copland, Jonathan Richards and Andrew Walker; Editor: Margaret Zucker, Cedar Centre, Toowoomba 2010.

fellah? Brother belonging to me'. They one and all answered 'they knew nothing about the murder'. He also enquired 'where Pimpilly?' this they also confessed that they knew nothing whatever about him. Mr Dowling then said, 'If you do not tell me, I will shoot the lot of yous'. Still they all remained silent. Mr Dowling and the others then set to work and put an end to many of them, not touching the 'Gins' and young fry. This I know is true as I helped first to burn the bodies and then to bury them. A most unpleasant undertaking! But as I was only a 'Jackaroo' on 'Cheshunt' station at the time, I had to do what I was told.[229]

A similar massacre took place on a neighbouring station later on the same day. Eventually Pimpilly was captured and killed. He had killed Dowling after receiving a vicious beating for not providing his master and horse with water.[230]

[228] Australian Dictionary of Biography (1972), Vol. 4, p. 99.

[229] Queensland historical manuscripts – *Vol 2 'Original Reminiscences of South West Queensland'* by E.O. Hobkirk, NLA, MS 3460.

[230] ibid.

The authors introduce their scholarly work as follows, "This book represents a condensation of over two years of systematic research of manuscripts, newspapers and government documents. It is based on a selection from a wide range of archival records ... However, this is the most comprehensive effort to date in drawing together historical material relating to dispossession in the region."[35] Not satisfied with that

[35] Copland: 2010 p 3.

overdrawn statement, these learned gentlemen go on to make this breathtaking gasconade, "*One Hour More Daylight* provides far too much evidence to sustain an argument that there has been a 'fabrication of aboriginal history'."[36]

The first aspect of this publication to note is that Jonathan Richards is one of the three authors. Turning to the above quote of Hobkirk's, Copland et al use the word 'Gins' the manuscript says 'lubras'. It is an error; perhaps, it was a typographical error? There is no analysis of the source material or the incident. It appears in their book as a recital might be found in a deed, pleadings, lineage, or a Norse saga. The authors seem to treat it as folklore, thus beyond scrutiny even when it may be a false or unsubstantiated source. They say they made a systemic search of newspapers but do not refer to the numerous reportages of the incident that appeared in the newspapers of Queensland, New South Wales and Victoria.[37]

In 2008, the University of Queensland Press published a book called *The Secret War: A True History of Queensland's Native Police* by Jonathon Richards which appears to be based on his above thesis of 2005. The book was reprinted in 2017. The relevant section is quoted as follows:

> One credible account of a killing perpetrated by squatters and their employees, is found in the reminiscences of

---

[36] Copland: 2010 p 4.
[37] See Appendix G

Edward Hobkirk, an employee at Dowling's Station on the Bulloo River. It is unclear when Hobkirk actually wrote this account, but the other records in the file cover the period from 1870 to 1923 and he gave his manuscript to William Gall at the Home Secretary's Office in 1922.[47] According to Hobkirk, grazier Vincent Dowling's reported in writing to the nearest Native Police (probably Bungil Creek near Roma) after his brother John ('Jack') Dowling was killed in 1864 by his 'pet blackboy'. Hobkirk said Dowling was told to 'take what measures he thought best to revenge the murder,' so 'all the men in the neighbourhood' were assembled and 'armed with revolvers and rifles' before the local Aboriginal tribe was mustered at gunpoint. Hobkirk admitted he helped bury the bodies that Dowling and others shot at several camps. One source says Vincent Dowling 'subsequently became a terror to the blacks'.[48]

[47] E.O. Hobkirk, Original *Reminiscences of South West Queensland*, National Library of Australia, Manuscript MS 3460, Volume 2.

[48] Charles F Maxwell, Australian men of Mark 1788 – 1888 Vol. 1 (Sydney: Charles F Maxwell, no date), 385.

When you compare and contrast his thesis with the above quote from 2017 reprint, you will find that he has rearranged the text slightly. However, he still maintains that John Dowling was killed in 1864 and Hobkirk was an employee of Vincent Dowling notwithstanding, the contradictory statements made by Richards in his 2006 collaborative work in *One Hour More Daylight*. So, the blatant errors of the thesis and the lack of critical analysis of the source material are transferred into Richards' published work, *The Secret War*. So much for authentic, accurate, and honest scholarship and tight professional editorial control alleged by university publishing houses. Richards is primarily writing about the Queensland Native Police but note this bold statement, '... the infamous force created to kill Aboriginal and Torres Strait people in Queensland'.[38] So, a simplistic take on why Richards would include John Dowling's death is that if the Native Police cannot do the job, then the squatter can make application for a licence to kill and he will be authorised as Vincent Dowling was, to carry out the extermination policy. The sheer preposterousness of the statement is beyond belief and not a shred of evidence is offered to prove that the Queensland Government ever authorised and directed Vincent Dowling to kill Bulloo River Blacks or that the Native Police were a state-run extralegal organisation killing Aborigines. Aborigines were killed and so were settlers and police in the many collisions that occurred on the Queensland frontier. What I said about Richards's thesis applies equally to his published work by University of Queensland Press.

Raymond Evans in 2010, contributing to *Passionate histories: myth, memory and Indigenous Australia* at Part One: massacres, with, *1. The country has another past: Queensland and the History Wars*[39] also draws upon the Titus Oates of Australian history, EO Hobkirk, who should be called

---

[38] Richards, *The Secret War, 2017 p 4.*
[39] *Passionate histories: myth, memory and Indigenous Australia* edited by Frances Peters-Little, Ann Curthoys and John Docker, ANU E Press and Aboriginal History Incorporated 2010.

Hobkirk the Liar, with the old familiar refrain:

In 1865, for instance, EO Hobkirk, 'an old identity of South Western Queensland' was present at a mass killing of Aborigines on the Bulloo River after an Aboriginal worker, described as a 'pet black boy', murdered John Dowling, the manager of Thouringowa Station. His brother, Vincent gathered a white posse to secure the culprit, but when local Aborigines would not provide information – to quote Hobkirk: Mr. Dowling then said, 'if you do not tell me I will shoot the lot of yous'. Still they remained silent. Mr. Dowling and the others then set to work and put an end to many of them, not touching the 'gins' and young fry. This I know to be true as I helped first to burn the bodies and then to bury them. A most unpleasant undertaking! But as I was only a 'Jackaroo' on 'Cheshunt' station at the time, I had to do what I was told.[43] Vincent Dowling had earlier been a pioneering cattleman on the Upper Darling River in 1859. His head stockman, John Edward Kelly later provided graphic descriptions of atrocities visited by white settlers on the local Aboriginal peoples. 'We feel perfectly certain that we have not exaggerated one single statement we have made', Kelly concluded his account: 'We have seen the bones'.[44]

[43] Copland et al 2006: 77–78; Richards 2008: 67.

[44] The Stockwhip, 22 April 1876; Maryborough Chronicle, 9 May 1876; Evans, R 2009: 10.

Evans trots out the same old hackneyed source uncritically. Hobkirk is an inappropriate source. No attempt is made to address the other material that is available. Evans adopts a studious ardour to avoid any material that might question or threaten the leftist view that a white man massacred Aborigines. What is of interest though, is Evans' novel attempt to baluster Hobkirk's credibility by the juxtaposition of a totally irrelevant quote from Vincent Dowling's head stockman, JE Kelly. It is a variation of the guilt by association technique. Kelly says he had heard reports of atrocities against Aborigines and then gives a general description of these activities. I fail to see the relevance of Kelly's statement, since John Dowling was killed in 1865 long after the period Kelly is describing and he further says that whilst he was in the area working for Vincent Dowling no atrocities were committed by Dowling or his staff. However, if a quote has to be given perhaps the following might be fair and adequate:

> We are speaking (says the writer) of the year 1859. The blacks on the Darling had been most barbarously murdered by our early predecessors, hunted like kangaroos or wild dogs, wherever they were known to exist. ... driving him home, and there "stretching" and flogging him as already described. This was about the extent of the punishment inflicted upon the blacks when we first took up our abode on the Darling — that is by the sheep-men. ... Although we never saw a black shot or "stretched"— for the simple reason that no man living dare do such a thing in our presence — still we feel perfectly certain that we have not exaggerated one single statement that we have made. We have seen 'the bones;"[40]

[40] *Maryborough Chronicle*, 9 May 1876.

The next attempt at dealing with the murder of John Dowling may be found in Timothy Bottoms' book *Conspiracy of Silence* published in 2013. His portrayal of the incident is as follows:

> In 1864, Jones, Sullivan and Molesworth Greene established Bulloo Downs Station (c. 113 kilometres south-west of the future Thargomindah, and 20 kilometres north of the NSW border). The following year, the owner of Fort Bourke Station on the Darling River, Captain John (Jack) Dowling, formed Ardock Station and not long afterwards, his brother, Vincent James Dowling, took up Thargomindah Station.[13] Later in 1865, while managing his brother's station, John Dowling was out on the run mustering, and was beaten to death with a waddy while sleeping beside his campfire. His 'tame black boy', 'Pimpilly', had sought revenge for a beating he received from Dowling for not promptly bringing water to his 'master' and his horse when so ordered. A Kooma descendant, Hazel McKellar, recalled: 'As a reprisal ... [they] found the tribe camped on the eastern side of the river, chased them towards the hills [Grey Range], shooting them down as they ran.'[14] This occurred at Thouringowa Waterhole on the Bulloo River (rough halfway, south-west, between Thargomindah and Bulloo Downs). EO Hobkirk was in Vincent Dowling's white posse that went in search of the alleged perpetrator. He described how they had corralled a camp of Kullilli, and Dowling had demanded to know who had killed his brother, but the Kullilli confessed that they knew nothing about the murder, to which Dowling responded:
>
> > 'If you do not tell me, I will shoot the lot of yous'.

Still they all remained silent. Mr Dowling and the others then set to work and put an end to many of them not touching the lubras and young fry. This I know is true as I helped first to burn the bodies and then to bury them. A most unpleasant undertaking! but as I was only a 'Jackaroo' on Cheshunt station at the time, I had to do what I was told. Later in the day the party went to another camp of blacks, about 20 miles down the river and there again shot about the same number.[15]

Dowling continued to terrorise the Aboriginal population to avenge his brother's murder, while employing Aboriginal labour.[16] The bookkeeper at Norley Station (c.30 kilometres north of Thargomindah) recalled that in 1911, there was an old Aboriginal there who: ... claimed to be the sole survivor of the massacre. A piccaninny at the time, his mother had hidden him under bark in a hole in the floor of the gunyah. The troopers had burnt the camp there and crawled out later.[17]

It was reported later that nearly 300 people were killed in this incident. Although the numbers may well have been an exaggeration, it was nevertheless a sizeable killing spree.

[13] J St Pierie,'18. Some Information on the History of South West Qld,' in *Warrego and South West Queensland Historical Society Collection of Papers, Cunnamulla and District*, Vol.1, 1969, p.2 (of paper).

[14] H McKellar, *Matya-mundu: a history of the Aboriginal people of South West Queensland,* Cunnamulla Australian Native Welfare Association, 1984, p.57.

[15] E O Hobkirk, *Queensland historical manuscripts* -Vol.2 *'Original Reminiscences of South West Queensland'*, NLA MS3460, (1922) pp. 3-4. Cheshunt Station is located 20 kilometres south-west

of Taro, or c.100 kilometres west of Dalby.

16   Hobkirk, NLA MS3460. Hobkirk noted: 'We found it hard to prevent the few that were employed on the station from ... [running away into the ranges] ... as they were so scared at what had taken place that we had to lock them up in the Hut – that was used as a store[,] for a short time.' p.4.

17   G Cooch (bookkeeper at Norley in 1911) cited by St Pierie, History of South West Queensland,' in *Warrego and South West Queensland Historical Society Collection of Papers, Cunnamulla and District*, Vol.1, 1969, p.3 (of paper).[41]

Timothy Bottoms holds a degree of Doctor of Philosophy and is a professional historian. As an historian his first step should have been to consult the *Australian Dictionary of Biography* (ADB) and he would have found an entry for Vincent James Dowling[42] which would have alerted him to the inaccuracy of the St. Pierie's version because it would have shown that John Dowling was not the owner of Fort Bourke.

The above extract from Bottoms' book is a melange of two sources (St. Pierie and Hobkirk) cherry-picked to invent a credible historical event that never occurred. It contains errors and omissions woven in a way to breath a fictional dimension to a past event such as John Dowling's murder. The first and by far the greatest omission is the failure to identify the 1865 press reports of John Dowling's death

---

[41]   Bottoms, Timothy *Conspiracy of Silence Queensland's Frontier Killing Times*, Allen & Unwin, 2013 pp 63-64.

[42]   First published in hardcopy in *Australian Dictionary of Biography*, Volume 4, (MUP), 1972. "Early in 1859 (Vincent) Dowling drove 1200 Hereford heifers to establish a station on the Darling, which became known as Fort Bourke.

and to make an appraisal of them. The second is his failure to critically assess the source material he finally acted on. For instance, the Gooch/St. Pierie version, was first written down by J St. Pierie in 1969 who got it from Gooch, a bookkeeper, who only arrived at Norley station, which is near Thargomindah, in 1911, 46 years after the event. Gooch was not an eyewitness. He can only have acquired his version by hearsay, local gossip. Bottoms then adds some pepper and salt by saying that: "A Kooma descendant, Hazel McKellar, recalled: 'As a reprisal … [they] found the tribe …'." Hazel McKellar was not an eye witness. The use of the word 'recalled' suggests she brought (a fact, event, or situation) back into her mind; remembered it. She wrote a book that quoted Gooch/St. Pierie and failed to give any citation for the quote. Her work can only be viewed as a very poor secondary source of doubtful veracity and honesty. Bottoms further distorts the sources by adding, "Dowling continued to terrorise the Aboriginal population to avenge his brother's murder, while employing Aboriginal labour." Hobkirk was an employee of the Messrs Sams on the Cheshunt station. He did not work for Vincent Dowling and therefore, would not know what labour problems Vincent had, if indeed he had any. Furthermore, Bottoms says, "Cheshunt Station is located 20 kilometres south-west of Taro, or c.100 kilometres west of Dalby". There is no town called Taro; it is Tara Qld 4421. Circa 100 kilometres west of Dalby would equate with the town of Moonie. This makes Bottoms' version even more absurd. The only integrity that Hobkirk's version has and it is very little, is that Cheshunt Station was a neighbouring station to VJ Dowling's Thuringowa Station, not approximately 700 kilometres from Thargomindah as Moonie is.

That appears to be the total historical treatment of the murder of John Dowling and the aftermath by professional historians. I just want to end this chapter with a quick overview of the above analysis of the academic treatment of John Francis Dowling's murder by one or more Aborigines. As I opined in the Preface to this book, some will see this book as just another brick hurled in the History Wars squabble. I do not. The point I am trying to make is that the writing of history is simply a matter of honesty and accuracy on the part of the historian who is further duty bound to discover and bring to notice any and all sources of knowledge relating to the historical event under study. Furthermore, the information or evidence must be initially assessed as to its worthiness or probity by an agreed set of rules for evaluating its admissibility. These sorts of ground rules should be above concepts of conformity to prevailing political or fashionable standards. I have always thought that was the case. But it seems that history somehow or other ends up being the plaything of newly emerging groups in society who seem to demand the right to tell their story in their own way. Well may they say, we have that right and who would deny them their campfire songs and stories. However, a society or a nation is not just a bunch of social media jerks, who have emerged from the chrysalis of social justice, flimflamming on their cell phones. Standards of academic excellence must be preserved and maintained even in the face of the social justice warrior. If you want to write a history from the point of view of a political or social belief then say so.

3

The Murder

To summarise Chapter One above: The deceased, John Francis Dowling, gentleman, 29 years of age, born 1836 in the colony of NSW, was murdered on the night of 13 June 1865 by one or more Aborigines. Death was by blunt force trauma to the head caused by, in this case, a large stick which crushed in the skull, probably inflicted while the deceased slept. A large stick was found, bloody, and with portion of the deceased's hair sticking to it at the scene of the crime. The place of death was the Paroo River, Queensland.[43] The body was found by Messrs Podmore and Hall, the search party, seven weeks after death. The last person to see the deceased alive was his guide, an Aborigine called Waddy Galo of the Kullilli tribe from the Bulloo River area. Mr Dowling appeared to be making a route along the Paroo River from Caiwarroo to where the Paroo joins the Darling

---

[43] Refer Death Certificate, Appendix A.

River at place called Mount Murchison Station. It appears the deceased travelled four full days, a distance of 40 miles or 65 kilometres and had entered a waterless tract of country apparently, at fault as to his position. Consequently, he sought the assistance of the local indigenous people of this area, who could tell him "no more about the springs." As the deceased property was found intact and nothing removed or stolen, it does not appear the deceased was killed for his property or goods. The horses, seven weeks after the incident, had not been found.

The first question to be settled is who had jurisdiction over the death of the deceased? Since he died in Queensland, then it would have been a matter for the Queensland magistrates and police. The immediate priority seems to have been the return of Mr John Dowling's remains to his brother, Vincent. What transpired after Messrs Podmore and Hall returned to civilisation with the remains of John Francis Dowling is not clear other than reporting their finds to Vincent Dowling and then the rest of the world. The conventional approach would have been to write or communicate with the nearest Magistrate or Native Police camp for the purposes of holding an inquest on the body of John Dowling to determine when, where and how and by what means the deceased came to his death. No record of an inquest or any subsequent actions have been found to date, other than the recording of John Dowling's death by Charles Claudius Carter, District

Registrar of Deaths in the Warrego District on 19 November 1866 at Charleville on the information of IP Lamb of 140 McLeary Street, Sydney.[44]

As to the perpetrator of John Dowling's death, the obvious suspect was Waddy Galo but why would he murder his employer? Since the incident falls in that period of time when most Aborigines were considered myall or uncivilised, tribal reasons need to be considered. Insults and injuries to wild Aborigines by careless or unmindful whites may not have seemed obvious or apparent at the time nor indeed, hurtful because of ignorance and lack of sensitivity to Black ways. Determining precisely what actually was the gross act of transgression is an area of sheer speculation. Moreover, Aborigines killing an offending party, white or black, was a legitimate tribal remedy for breaches of aboriginal etiquette and/or social customs. On the other hand, the colonial justice system viewed Aborigines killing white settlers as prima facie unlawful. The *Brisbane Courier* offered the following:

> Mr Dowling was murdered; he was accompanied only by one black guide; murder under these circumstances is an unusual thing. If they were afterwards joined by other Blacks, of course the case is different. Mr Dowling was in search of water, and an entry found in his journal, says that the Blacks refused to show him the

---

[44] The identity of IP Lamb is undiscoverable; equally, McLeary Street is unclear. However, Walter Lamb JP lived at Macleay Street, Sydney, Sands Directory 1866 p 267. Walter was the brother of J deV Lamb and Edward William Lamb, Chief Commissioner of Crown Lands, Queensland, 1962-1867.

springs, (this) will be taken as conclusive evidence that they killed him in order to preserve the small supply of water necessary for the existence of the tribe.

Another possible transgression was John Dowling taking a Bulloo tribesman into another tribal area, the Paroo. How much this worried Waddy Galo is hard to say but there are earlier instances of indigenous guides deserting their employers, not wanting to risk their lives in strange lands beyond their own country.[45] Duncan McIntyre related a similar story to Dowling's demise. A Mr Carlewis had coerced a blackfellow to accompany him to show him the country, and this man, not liking to go, persuaded four others to assist him in killing the two white men. Messrs Carlewis and McCulloch had their heads smashed in with waddies and tomahawks. McIntyre says he was shown the bodies by the Blacks and he was also told why and how it happened.[46] Anyway, Waddy Galo would have been a person of interest being the last person to have seen the deceased alive and the fact that he fled the scene of the crime, renders him even more of interest.

The only record of any action taken in regards to John Dowling's death is the account given by EO Hobkirk in his article of 1922, *The Murder of Mr John Dowling. Locality, Bulloo River Queensland*. The story consists of two major

---

[45] Hardy gives the example of Dicky deserting Howitt, *Lament for the Barkindji* 1976, p. 109.
[46] *Sydney Morning Herald*, 7 January 1865, p. 5.

parts, the finding of the body and the subsequent transactions and the second part, the identification and location of the perpetrator and his treatment. Hobkirk gives a version of the suspect:

> On the second night after leaving the station, Mr Dowling and he, camped without water for themselves or their horses. This annoyed Mr Dowling very much as he quite expected that there would be water as the (blackboy) had said there would. Mr Dowling struck him and called him names for deceiving him regarding the water. After lying down to rest and sleep with his saddle for a pillow (which was the custom among Bushmen), Pimpilly seeing that Mr Dowling was sound asleep hit him on the head with a heavy waddy that he had ready. Mr Dowling jumped up, grappled with him for a few seconds, and then fell down insensible. He then finished him off with several hits. His reason for killing him was that he was afraid that Mr Dowling would give him another hiding in the morning as he was doubtful when they would reach water. The following morning, he stripped the body of all its clothing gathered together anything that was of use to him then walked a long way and joined a camp of his tribe in the ranges. The above explanation is proof that the blackboy alone killed Mr John Dowling and by not a number of aboriginals as was stated by the Sydney newspapers at the time of the murder.

Oh! what a tangled web we weave when first we practice to deceive. The above version does not accord with 1865 press version except for the issue of the lack of water. The rest of the Hobkirk's particulars of the crime scene are at odds with the 1865 version. Be that as it may, the internal consistency of the story is breached when Hobkirk says, "camped without water for themselves or their horses." In the beginning of the story he says, "Not far away from the remains they discovered the three horses (mudfat). I believe still with their hobbles on and plenty of water and on good feed." The class show-off would no doubt put his hand up and say, "please sir, it could have rained after the murder." It could have, but Hobkirk not only hobbled the horses, he hobbled himself. Horses need food and water every twenty-four hours. So, they are like a camera. Asserting the horses were mudfat means they never lost condition and must have been on very lush country with easy access to a plentiful supply of water. Hobbling would have restricted the horses significantly and if they were abandoned on waterless country, "as he was doubtful when they would reach water," they would have wandered in search of water and rapidly lost condition given the stressful conditions they found themselves in: lack of water and no feed. A pool might form after rain but a plentiful supply of good grass would not grow over night. If an informant gives inconsistent evidence on material points then his credibility, honesty and veracity is non-existent and he must be rejected as an unreliable witness.

The Hobkirk version has two further major internal inconsistencies. He says, "the cook and myself were alone at the station (Cheshunt), the manager and the others being absent and not expected to return for some days." This is followed by the Pimpilly narrative. Then Hobkirk says, "Towards evening Mr Cameron who was in charge of Thouringowa in the place of the murdered gentleman returned home. I informed him of what had happened during his absence". Hobkirk does not offer an explanation of how or why the frame of reference is changed. The Pimpilly transaction commences on Cheshunt with the manager away. Then the frame of reference is changed abruptly to Thouringowa station when Cameron returns home, coincidently with the capture of Pimpilly, how convenient. There is an inconsistency here. It is more than just continuity. It suggests fabrication by the author; these types of mistakes occur most often when making up a story. Common to fiction stories but rare in factual statement of events or incidents. The other major inconsistency is Hobkirk writing:

> taking with him his pet blackboy (Pimpilly) and that was the last that was seen of him. He (Vincent) also enquired, "Where Pimpilly." This they also confessed "that they knew nothing whatever about him".

Then when Tom, the Murry River black turns up and says to Hobkirk:

> and that among them he had spied Pimpilly. (Hobkirk blurts out.) Who is Pimpilly? I enquired. Why don't you know. He was the boy who was with Mr Dowling and who is supposed to have killed him. Oh! I exclaimed!

Then we must collar him, Tom.

This reply by Hobkirk suggest he was unaware that Pimpilly was a person of interest. This inconsistency or error really drives home the point that the article is a piece of fiction and Hobkirk can't control the story he has written. A witness statement is a simple direct account of an incident told in strict chronological order, one fact at a time, step by step until the witness exhausts his knowledge of the incident.

Where were the police and why were they not involved? As to the Native Police, the following was observed in March 1865:

> This District (Warrego) has received no protection from the hostile natives—with which it swarms—except a small force of Native Police, under Lieutenant Lambert, who, although a very meritorious officer, finds it impossible with his force to guard efficiently a district extending in length to 600 miles.[47]

Charles Henry Lambert described himself as a Sub-inspector of the Maranoa Mounted Patrol; and was in Roma on 6 May 1864, in charge of the Native Police.[48] On 31 December 1864 the stockholders in the District of Warrego wrote to the Colonial Secretary seeking to have enhanced or reinforced Lt Lambert on the Yo Yo and to established another section (of Native Police) on the lower Warrego and Paroo where Blacks were extremely troublesome. Premier

---

[47] *Rockhampton Bulletin and Central Queensland Advertiser*, 21 March 1865, p. 3.
[48] *Toowoomba Chronicle and Queensland Advertiser*, 20 July 1865, p. 2.

Herbert noted on the document: steps are about to be taken in accordance with the request of these gentlemen.[49] During the 1860s a Native Mounted Police camp was established on Yo Yo creek near Augathella. On 2 August 1865, a shepherd from Burenda Station, on the Warrego River was murdered. The Native Police were 150 miles away at Forest Vale.[50] On 7 September 1865, Commissioner Seymour wrote to the Colonial Secretary as follows:

> I have the honour to recommend that, as the Districts of the Lower Warrego and Barcoo rivers are so remote, the patrol authorised for those districts as well as the constables stationed in Charleville should be placed under the charge of an Inspector and should this meet with the approval of the Government, I would further recommend that Mr Sub-inspector Lambert, NP (now in the District) be promoted.[51]

On 19 September 1865, Seymour sought approval to incur an outlay of £500 to purchase additional horses for the new native police patrol of the Warrego and Barcoo Rivers, which was approved.[52] Seymour arrived at Roma on 20 January 1866, after a heavy journey through the rain with Inspector Lambert,

---

[49] QSL: A collection of papers on the history and other subjects to relating to Cunnamulla and district, prepared by members [of] the Warrego and South West Queensland Historical Society, Vol 3 p 174.
[50] *Brisbane Courier* 6 September 1865, p. 2. Near Mitchell Qld 4465.
[51] QSL: A collection of papers on the history and other subjects to relating to Cunnamulla and district, prepared by members [of] the Warrego and South West Queensland Historical Society, Vol. 3., p. 176.
[52] Ibid., p 176.

Mr Gilmore[53] and a large force of the Native Police.[54] The point I am trying to make is that the Queensland Police had limited resources and manpower at the time in the relevant area, the Paroo. The modern response would be a question of priorities and settled areas would be allocated resources over remote and unsettled areas. Therefore, it appears that no native police action was taken on the Paroo river relating to John Dowling's murder.

The next question is where was Vincent Dowling from late September 1865 to say 10 March 1866? Susan Emily Dowling, his sister married FA Powell at St Ann's, Ryde, NSW on 10 March 1866.[55] Furthermore, Vincent married on 4 May 1866 at St Peter's, Cook's River, NSW. Vincent gave his home address as Warpuelar, Fort Bourke, NSW. It seems unlikely that if Vincent Dowling was going to take punitive actions against the Bulloo River Blacks, it would be after these events. Apart from John Dowling's death, Vincent had another problem, his sheep in NSW had sheep scab and he was in breach of the Scab Act. Sheep scab is caused by mites living in sheep's fleeces or hair. The mites and their faeces cause intense itching which can lead to sheep: rubbing and scratching against fence posts and nibbling and biting at their fleeces. Vincent's solution to the problem was to obtain permission to move the sheep to his station on the Paroo. In

---

[53] James Merry Gilmour was sworn in on November 25, 1865, Q Police Book of Names 1864-1974.
[54] *Brisbane Courier,* 2 February 1866, p. 3.
[55] *Sydney Morning Herald,* 13 March 1866, p. 1.

August 1865, he obtained permission from the Queensland government to do so under the supervision of Mr Mayne, the Scab-inspector for Warrego.[56] This is a description of the droving of the sheep into Queensland:

> The weather is still hot, without the faintest sign of rain, station after station is being deserted, and in a month's time there will be a general turnout. I speak of country downwards from Culla Mulla, and even there, though there is water, feed is alarmingly scarce. Six or eight thousand of Mr Vincent Dowling's sheep moved from the Culla Burra to the Paroo, passing up the Warrego from the Company's cattle station. They had but three or four small waterholes to call at, but instead of watering and passing on, giving other travellers a chance, the gentleman in charge has literally ruined what little water we had on the road, staying two or three days where he had no right to stay but one. The consequence is, all communication with Bourke in a few days will cease. This conduct has greatly annoyed everyone here, and justly too. The blacks are giving trouble at West's, on the Yougha. The troopers have not been yet to Mr Birkett's, expected daily, December 27.[57]

After reading the 1866 diary of Vincent Dowling it is very clear that Vincent took an active part in managing the sheep drive. The evidence suggests he travelled extensively from Bourke to Caiwarroo making arrangements for the sheep and

---

[56] *Darling Downs Gazette and General Advertiser* 19 August 1865 p 3.
[57] *Maitland Mercury and Hunter River General Advertiser* 9 January 1866, p. 3.

hiring men to wash the sheep. Moreover, the above shows how bad the conditions were regarding the weather and the availability of surface water on the Paroo and surrounding area. Therefore, risking white men's lives, in chasing round the countryside after murderous Blacks to avenge his brother death would be foolhardy and hardly a sensible venture by an experience explorer like Vincent Dowling. Finally, at the time, Vincent was trying to recruit senior staff for his pastoral business:

> WANTED, a thoroughly practical working SHEEP OVERSEER, for a Station near Bourke, Darling River must be a married man of sober years. Wife to act as HUTKEEPER to Superintendent. None but men of experience need apply. Salary, £150 per annum, with the usual allowances. Applications, with testimonials, references to be sent to Vincent Dowling, Esq., Bourke.[58]

---

[58] *Sydney Morning Herald,* 31 October & 8 November 1865, p. 8.

4

The Massacre?

The word massacre means "an indiscriminate and brutal slaughter of many people." There is no body count required before one may choose to use the word and like all words now found in the social justice lexicon, it has become part of the black armband brigade's hyperbole. Almost de rigeur, when any frontier Aborigines are found to have been killed by whites or their hired gunslingers, to describe it as a massacre. There is in my view, no valid evidence of a massacre of any Bulloo River Blacks by Vincent Dowling in the year of our lord 1865, either in the company of Hobkirk or without Hobkirk. Certainly, a number of white men died from thirst and other misadventures including death at the hands of Aborigines.

Turning now to Vincent James Dowling, who is said to have led an avenging posse that massacred the Bulloo Blacks sometime in last three months of 1865. The only evidence that Vincent led an avenging posse is given by EO Hobkirk, who I would call an infuriating, namedropping, lickspittle of a gossip who had all the arrogance of an ignoramus and none of the caution and honesty of a scholar. According to Hobkirk, the sole and principle reason Vincent Dowling is alleged to have taken action in the matter of his brother's death was because: "I was informed that he (Mr Dowling) had written to the Queensland government authorities concerning the murder and the reply was to take what measures he thought best to revenge the murder as there was no native police at that time in the District to see to the matter." What does this sentence mean? The operative part seems, "to take what measures he thought best to revenge the murder." Revenge means: inflict hurt or harm on someone for an injury or wrong done to oneself. I suppose the definition of revenge that we are all familiar with is the biblical injunction: an eye for an eye. The English criminal law that prevailed in the colony of Queensland at that time, 1865, did not allow or authorise revenge killings. There also was no bounty fee payable, by the Queensland government for Aborigines killed, to those who may have produced a pair of hands or ears as proof of death. In fact, it was illegal to kill or harm Aborigines as the whites who killed the Aborigines at Myall Creek soon found out under Governor Gipps' rule. Seven white men were hanged on 18 December 1838 for murdering Aborigines. Therefore, under what authority or power did the Queensland government purport to authorise Vincent Dowling to kill Aborigines? Any student of Australian colonial history should be familiar with the *Maria* incident when 25 survivors of the wreck were massacred by Aborigines on the Coorong, South Australia. Governor Gawler authorised and directed Major O'Halloran as follows: when "you have identified any number, not exceeding three, of the actual murderers ... you will deliberately and formally cause sentence of death to be executed by shooting or hanging" them, which he did. The error Gawler made was not instructing O'Halloran to arrest the suspected Aborigines and have them brought to Adelaide to be put upon their trial for the murder of the survivors and, if convicted, then executed. The Colonial Office advised "that their summary execution was an act of murder. The Commissioner of Police and those present helping him were guilty as principals and the Governor an accessory before the fact. They could be indemnified only by an Act of Parliament or by a pardon under the Great Seal." Any diligent scholar of Australian colonial history would have realised that this statement by Hobkirk was balderdash and could not be accepted as an honest and accurate statement of fact. Hobkirk could not be a valid historical source for the allegations he made against Vincent Dowling and the Queensland government of the day that Vincent Dowling had been authorised and directed to revenge kill Aborigines, because the statement is without credibility, integrity, reliability, and without any foundation in law whatsoever.

Let us now turn to the event Hobkirk says he took part

in. Hobkirk says John Dowling was at the Dowling's Bulloo station, Thouringowa prior to his death and travelled down the Bulloo with his Bulloo black servant, when he was killed by the servant and that John Dowling's body was subsequently found on the Bulloo by Mr Sams and his search party. As a consequence, Hobkirk (unarmed), in the company of Vincent Dowling and others, who were armed, went to the nearest Blacks' camp on the Bulloo and shot and killed many adult males because they failed to assist Dowling in his enquiries into his brother's death. Later in the same day, Dowling then moved onto the next Bulloo camp and there again shot about the same number.

This statement was made by Hobkirk in 1922, 57 years after the event when Hobkirk was approximately 77 years old. The facts given by Hobkirk in 1922 do not reconcile with facts of John Dowling's death as related at the time of his death.

Facts	1865 Version	1922 Hobkirk
Deceased Victim	John Dowling	John Dowling
Departure Point	Caiwarroo Paroo	Thouringowa Bulloo
Guide	Waddy Galo	Pimpilly
Reason for travel	Cutting a road	Exploration
Destination	Mount Murchison	Menindee
Duration of travel	Four full days	Not clear/not stated
Search party	Messrs Podmore & Hall	Mr Sams & stockman
Duration of search	Travelled 30 or 40 miles from Paroo	2 days 60 miles from Cheshunt Bulloo
Place of Death	Paroo River Queensland	Bulloo River Queensland
Date of Death	13 June 1865	Not clear/not stated
Environment	Waterless track of country, lost	Good country couldn't locate water
Manner of death	Single blow to head crushing skull	Blow to head struggle then several blows to skull
Reason for death	unknown	To avoid further beatings
Crime scene	Camp site undisturbed	Camp site looted
Perpetrator	unknown	Pimpilly
Horses	Not found	Nearby mudfat plenty of water good feed

There is no reason to question or challenge the version given in 1865 by informants who were involved with the recovery of John Dowling's body; namely, the Dowling family and their agents and servants. Hobkirk's article of 1922 has many of the characteristics of what is called a voluntary false confession. Principally, the main motive for such activity is that the actor/author is seeking notoriety, celebrity, publicity, recognition and in the case of Hobkirk money. Police rarely release the full details of a crime scene relating to murder as it is a way of weeding out false confessions. Where a person comes forward and voluntarily confesses to a crime, his status as a suspect is determined by the level of particulars that he can give in relation to the commission of the crime such as a detailed and accurate description of the physical evidence and method of killing at the scene of the crime. The most outrageous piece of evidence Hobkirk gives is:

> Not far away from the remains they discovered the three horses (mudfat). I believe still with their hobbles on and plenty of water and on good feed. It was rather strange that they did not make their way back to the station. Had they done so, it would have foretold a tale.

This statement is totally inconsistent with the original version on many levels. On the 1865 version, the horses were never found. Moreover, John Dowling was lost in a waterless tract of country. The reader may also wish to note that Hobkirk says that John Dowling's kit and equipment were looted when in fact the original crime scene was simply abandoned after the murder, not disturbed or looted. Furthermore, the reader may care to peruse a news item contained in the *Gympie Times and Mary River Mining Gazette* of 10 November 1910, *A Northern Territory Tragedy Port Darwin. November 4*. Hobkirk's version bears a closer resemblance to the circumstances of that story than it does to John Dowling's death:

Gympie Times

The remains had been picked clean of flesh by wild dogs. The head was not found until late in the afternoon, and nearly three hundred yards away from the first found remains. Torn pieces of clothing, a pocket knife, a waterbag, and a Browning revolver were found lying around. His three hobbled horses were found, but no trace of the owner.[59]

Hobkirk

they discovered the remains consisting only of bones, and a scull (sic, skull), which had been dragged about in various directions by the native dogs. There were also the remains of two saddles and a pack saddle, a revolver and a pair of riding boots belonging to Mr Dowling. Not far away from the remains they discovered the three horses (mudfat). I believe still with their hobbles on and plenty of water and on good feed.

Therefore, it may be safely said that Hobkirk's article is a piece of fiction written to entertain. If it were to be held out or represented as a factual record or the description of an historical event, then it must be said to be a pack of lies, a fabrication and a deliberate falsification of the historical record and an untrue piece of yellow journalism.

Like all journalists, Hobkirk never let the facts get in the way of a good story. In December 1926, Hobkirk wrote an article for the *Queenslander* called *The Warrego*. This piece perhaps might be considered as a brief description of his

---

[59] Abridged by the author.

time in the Warrego District. He says: "Knowing that district from 1865 to 1888 I shall describe what I remember about it." Nota bene, this man was aged 81 years old in 1926, writing about events occurring from 1865 onwards, sixty odd years after the events. Hobkirk relates as follows:

> In 1865 Inspector Gilmore was engaged with a search party, of which he was the leader, for traces of the lost expedition (Leichhardt), and at a place called Wantala be found some human remains. These, however, turned out to be aboriginal.
>
> I knew Inspector Gilmore well at the time he was contemplating going on this trip, and was asked to make one of the party. There was too much to do at the station at the time, so I declined. Inspector Gilmore's party consisted of himself, his second in command —a white sergeant—and five black troopers. I do not know how far the party went, but do know that they discovered the remains before mentioned—aboriginal remains. The weather was then very dry, and supplies ran very low, so the party turned homeward.
>
> Inspector Gilmore attempted another search to try to discover signs of Leichhardt's expedition in 1871. I might have joined him this trip, but was on the road, travelling in charge of 1000 head of mixed cattle from Juandah and Carrebah, of the Dawson River, the cattle having been purchased by Messrs. Lamb and Sams Bros., of Norley, the destination of the stock.

The reader is asked to note that the year referred to above is 1865. Hobkirk in his article of 1922, *The Murder of Mr*

John Dowling. Locality, Bulloo River Queensland says, "there was no native police at that time (1865) in the District to see to the matter." Gilmore, whose name was James Merry Gilmour, was sworn in on 25 November 1865 and spent his initial period travelling with Commissioner Seymour and was in Roma in January 1866. What Hobkirk has related above is incorrect, see *The Brisbane Courier,* 5 April 1871 which reproduced the inspector's account of his discovery of aboriginal remains in 1871 not 1865. The second voyage undertaken by Gilmour was undertaken in late 1871.[60] Gilmour turned up in the Warrego in about mid 1866 when he seized a dray load of grog.[61]

The point is that in 1922 when it suits his story (*The Murder of John Dowling*), the police are not available on the Bulloo in 1865. In 1926, when he is showing off his skill and reputation as a bushman in 1865 on the Bulloo, he says the police asked him to join their patrol notwithstanding, it was against police regulations to take a civilian on a police patrol.[62]

In 1922 he writes in *The Murder of Mr John Dowling. Locality, Bulloo River Queensland:*

After the massacre (late 1865) the whole tribe of blacks

---

[60] *Ballarat Star* 17 January 1872.
[61] *Brisbane Courier* 15 September 1866, p. 6.
[62] 11. The officers are not to allow any person unconnected with the Native Police Force to interfere with or accompany them, or give orders to any of the troopers under their command. Native Police Regulations as published in Queensland Government Gazette (10 March 1866).

left the river frontage and that locality and went miles away out in the ranges and elsewhere. We found it hard to prevent the few that were employed on the station from doing likewise as they were so scared at what had taken place that we had to lock them up in the hut that was used as a store for a short time. For many months there was not a single black man to be seen for miles around excepting the few already mentioned ...

In 1923 he writes in *Impersonating an Aboriginal*:

> At this time (1867) I was living on Cheshunt cattle station, on the Bulloo River, where a corrobboree was about to take place. Being a good mimic, with both voice and actions, I planned, to impersonate a blackfellow, and take part in the corrobboree ... I joined the aboriginal's, about, 300 all told. The larger portion were men; they only took part in the actual corroboree. Some of the gins contributed the music by clapping boomerang's together, keeping good time and singing their gibberish in their thin, but melodious voices;

There is more:

> The white spectators consisted of Mr Sams, (my boss), Mr V Dowling of Thuringowa station (now Thargomindah station), Mr A Sullivan of Bulloo Downs, the men working on Cheshunt station, and some from other stations in the district. The performance lasted about two hours. Once, when I was quite to the front, I heard Mr Dowling say, " Where is H(obkirk)? and Green, the cook, who, of course, was among the spectators, said something about my having to go off somewhere after some cattle, and having taken Dickey

with me, so could not be present, at the same time H(obkirk) was within a few yards of him, and yet was not detected.

When the performance was over, I stepped out of the crowd of blacks, and going up to Mr Dowling, said "Good evening, Mr Dowling." "By Jove! he exclaimed, "why, it's H(obkirk)! Well, you are a caution, and no mistake." Needless to add, the others also were astonished at my complete disguise, and I was greatly complimented on my achievement by all who had witnessed the corroboree. So, I can flatter myself that my impersonation of an aboriginal was a decided success.

No greater skite could be found beyond the black stump, other than Baron Munchausen. Twelve months prior to this, Dowling and Sams had led a group of bushwhackers who were said to have wiped out the entire adult male population of the Bulloo River Blacks only to find that in 1867, 300 initiated, full blood adult males are back before the Bulloo Butchers to showcase one of their important cultural events, a corrobboree.

Hobkirk was obsessed with the Dowling family because of their fame in the pastoral industry of South West Queensland and elsewhere. Hobkirk writing in *Ladies in the Never Never*, made the following observations:

> I am not sure which of the two arrived out there first as I was absent from the district during 1869 and '70 and part of 71 arriving back in August of that year in

charge of 1000 head of mixed cattle for Norley Station a neighbouring to Thargomindah and Ardock station where the two ladies were respectively located meeting first Mrs Dowling the young wife of Mr Vincent Dowling of Cox and Dowling, at Thargomindah station and their two little children, girl and a baby boy-a girl coming between these two having been burnt in a black's camp when in charge of a black nurse.

Another great story, what the Dowling family thought of this drivel who knows? But it made great copy to learn that a high and mighty squatter, a high-born member of the Bunyip aristocracy, could not escape the clutches of Lady Luck who dealt the cards as she saw fit. Of course, as usual the statement is ambiguous, did the child survive with a horrible disfigurement or did the precious little thing perish through the negligence of some old lubra. Moreover, as the Bulloo Butcher, how many Aborigines did he massacre for causing the death of his beloved daughter? Mrs Dowling had the following children up until they left Thargomindah, Queensland in 1875 never to return:

Name	Date of Birth	District
Lilias Mary	9 March 1867	Newtown NSW
Ethel Maude	3 June 1869	Thargomindah Qld
Vincent Willoughby	19 May 1871	Thargomindah Qld
John George Henry	14 September 1874	Thargomindah Qld

Based on Hobkirk's statement, then the child burnt would be Ethel Maude. She coming between Lilias and Vincent Junior. However, the evidence suggests that Lilias Mary died on 1 May 1870 at Thargomindah, Queensland, aged 3 years and 51 days.[63] Her cause of death appears undiscoverable.[64] However, the following incident occurred in 1868 which may form the basis of Hobkirk's gobbledygook:

> The numerous friends of Mr and Mrs Vincent Dowling, of Culgoa, in this district will regret to learn that an accident befell Mrs Dowling a short time ago. It appears that the unfortunate lady was engaged superintending some household work, and in so doing set her dress on fire. She was instantly enveloped in flames and, but for the presence of mind of a blackboy engaged on the station, who succeeded in throwing a bucket of water over her, she would undoubtedly have perished on the spot. As it is, she sustained some severe burns, and it is to be feared is disfigured for life.[65]

When Vincent James Dowling died in 1903, several articles were written about his life. George Chale Watson (Commissioner for Crown Lands for the Warrego and Gregory South) writing in the *Queenslander* of 21 November 1903 had this to say about VJ Dowling, "Two of their children were burned to death, and a brother of Mr. Dowling's was killed by the blacks." In the *Queenslander* of 28 November 1903, it was observed as follows: "On two occasions tragic

---
[63] *Sydney Morning Herald*, 14 June 1870, p. 1.
[64] A search of the NSW and Queensland historical records of deaths drew a blank.
[65] *Sydney Morning Herald*, 5 March 1868, p. 4.

events occurred in Mr Dowling' family during his residence in this State. One was the murder of his brother, Mr John Dowling by blacks; the other the accidental death of his little daughter Lily through her frock catching fire at some embers of a blacks' fire." Even HP Ewart in her thesis seemed confused about the death of Lilias Mary Dowling, "Fanny endured many heartbreaks. The first-born child died before a daughter Ethel Maude was born in 1869."[66] Once again, we have a clear example of Hobkirk writing down gossip and hillbilly yarns he had heard, without regard to the truth, about a family he had an obsessive interest in.

Hobkirk says that Vincent Dowling called upon Mr Sams to search for his brother when he had men of his own employed on his Bulloo station, Thouringowa. Where was Mr Cameron, who mysteriously turned up and whisks Pimpilly away? Since he was 2IC of Thouringowa Station, why didn't he conduct the search for John Dowling? What actually was Mr Sams doing on his station of Cheshunt at the time of the incident? Hobkirk writing in the *Warrego* published in the *Queenslander* of 18 December 1926 says as follows:

> When I first met Mr Edmund Bignell in 1865 he resided at Dilallah station, but was on a visit to Coongoolah. This was before I reached the Bulloo. I was there with my employer, Mr Keate Sams. I was also at Claverton (Bigg and Geary's). Mr Sams having purchased 600

---

[66] Ewart, HP *Gentleman Squatters, self-made men and soldiers: Masculinities in nineteenth century Australia*, Thesis, University of Adelaide, July 2016, p. 128.

head of cattle at Coongoola and about 330 at Claverton.
I went out with them—my first droving trip.

The question I ask is how is one to read this paragraph? Does it mean Hobkirk travelled to Cheshunt Station with Keate Sams and picked the cattle up at Coongoolah and Claverton on the way and then took them onto Cheshunt or did he first go to Cheshunt and return for the cattle? Why is it important? Well Hobkirk alleges that Mr Sams and a stockman formed the search party to look for John Dowling. Then sometime after that they formed an avenging party led by Vincent which went off down the Bulloo River to sort the Blacks out, teach them a lesson, disperse them. If Hobkirk and Keate Sams were droving cattle from Coongoolah and Claverton, thirty odd miles north of Cunnamulla then onto Thargomindah sometime after August 1865, there would not be much of the year left for Dowling to travel from Bourke to the Bulloo, write to the Attorney-General for his licence to kill (mail was delivered by horse),[67] form and equip a posse of suitable white men at the height of summer and then round up and shoot the Blacks. Assuming of course, the Blacks loitered round the camps like sitting ducks. Even if the plain meaning of the paragraph is that the cattle were picked up on the way through to Cheshunt on the Bulloo and arriving there in August of 1865. Keate Sams would still have had on his hands a 1000 head of cattle which had to be

---

[67] Note what Bloxam said in 22 October 1864: to Brisbane, east by north, 700 miles, see above.

broken into to whatever portion of the run he chose to graze the cattle on, there were no fences in those days. It required men to stay with the cattle, tail them, which could involve months and months of hard riding and constant watching until they settled down. This is again another set of events that brings into question the credibility of Hobkirk and the absurdity of his scenario of Vincent Dowling conducting a revenge posse.

When a man is put upon his trial for criminal acts and outrages, he is entitled to call evidence or give evidence himself as to his good character. Vincent James Dowling stands accused of murdering a number of Aborigines on two separate occasions in late 1865. Is a man who has lived a blameless life likely to have indulged in such behaviour? Is a man who came from a family of lawyers with a solid English education and exposed to the high moral standards of Victorian England, a gentleman, likely to have indulged in such behaviour? As a judicial officer in New South Wales and Queensland would he have knowingly breached the law by murdering Aborigines? His accuser has a history of lying, fabricating stories, exaggeration, and an obsessional fascination with the Dowling family. In running and operating a pastoral enterprise in the wildness of Australia, the best one could hope for was that it would rain occasionally and the Blacks would leave you alone. Vincent Dowling would have been aware of the massacre of the Fraser Family, Hornet

Bank 1858 and of the Wills Family, Cullinlaringo, 1861 by the Blacks. As a businessman, what gain would he achieve in killing Aborigines? Vincent had firsthand experience of the Blacks himself as related in his 1863 incident of nearly being speared to death.

Although Vincent nearly died at the hands of Aborigines, he did not take any retaliatory action against them. He walked away not wanting to provoke or kill the Aborigines. Vincent showed much restraint and forbearance with the Aborigines. It was in his commercial and personal interest to include the Aborigines in his enterprise, when and where he could and thus encourage them away from destructive habits and acts that might damage or hinder his business.

In May 1864, he publicly said, "The blacks on the Paroo are the quietest I know in the colonies, and have never interfered with any men in my employ since the formation of the Paroo stations." On 28 February 1865 he publicly said, "I have no hesitation in again stating that the blacks of the Paroo and Lower Warrego are unexceptionably the quietest, most inoffensive, and likely to prove the most useful of any natives I have ever met with."

In January 1868, he donated to the Australian Museum two stone implements from the Paroo. Thus, demonstrating his interest in the culture of the Aborigines and also attempting to preserve some of it for future generations.[68]

---

[68] *Sydney Morning Herald*, 4 March 1868, p. 5.

On 2 May 1871, he was appointed by the Government a marriage celebrant of the District of Warrego under s18 of Marriage Act 1864, another sign of his good character and reputation.

On 5 June 1871, Vincent Dowling wrote to the Colonial Secretary requesting blankets for the Bulloo Blacks who had been settled for 7 years, "As the blacks here have been behaving well for a long time, I think they are deserving of some notice from the Government." The request was renewed on 15 August 1871, seeking blankets for station Blacks on the Bulloo, about 200 blankets were needed. Vincent wrote again to the Colonial Secretary on 25 June 1873 requesting blankets for the Blacks of the surrounding stations.[69]

The reader is referred to Appendix H where a massacre of Aborigines of the Kullilla tribe is listed as a creditable event between 1 January 1865 and 31 December 1865 based on the authoritative works of Bottoms 2013: 63-4 and McKellar 1984: 57. This site appears to operate under the aegis of the University of Newcastle, NSW[70] and is funded by the Australian Research Council[71], with the imposing injunction that "Only sites for which sufficient evidence can be found have been included in this website." Be that as it may, any fair-minded person reading the source material set out in

---

[69] QSL: A collection of papers on the history and other subjects to relating to Cunnamulla and district, prepared by members [of] the Warrego and South West Queensland Historical Society, Vol 3., p. 190.
[70] https://c21ch.newcastle.edu.au/colonialmassacres/
[71] Australian Research Council, Project ID: DP140100399.

detail in this book should be persuaded to the view that there was no massacre of Kullilli or Bulloo Blacks on the Bulloo River at any time during the year 1865. Why this allegation ever surfaced or has remained current is anybody's guess. The simple answer is that if you belong to the black armband school of Australian history, then the odd spear or boomerang hurled in anger really doesn't amount to a hill of beans in the real world of armed conflicts. They need casualty figures akin to WWI. On the other hand, there is an entrenched core of cockies out there who hold to the view that not a shot was fired in the European settlement of Australia. The reality in regards the Bulloo River Blacks, in 1865, is that no massacre took place either by white vigilantes or Native Police.

Summation

In 1972, a brave new world appeared on the horizon. Whitlam promised:

> We will abolish fees at universities and colleges of advanced education. We believe that a student's merit rather than a parent's wealth should decide who should benefit from the community's vast financial commitment to tertiary education. And more, it's time to strike a blow for the ideal that education should be free.[72]

With the election of Whitlam, hordes thronged the halls of learning tendering their merit badges and participation rates soared. A new world had arisen. Universities have enjoyed a boomtown experience that has gone from strength to strength. Forget the mainstream, what about real stories involving the underclasses which had been deliberately hidden or repressed by the conservatives? A slew of struggling, surging, sucklings threw themselves on the university bureaucracy

---

[72] Policy Speech for the Australian Labor Party, delivered by Gough Whitlam, at the Blacktown Civic Centre, in Sydney, on November 13, 1972.

demanding justice, more meaningful courses, more life skill courses on how to fill up a dole form or how to get a grant to study the architectural techniques of the Rufous rat. The answer was found in curriculum proliferation, the dumbing down of courses and the substitution of critical analysis by the employment of political correctness and social justice principles.

I opened this book about the History Wars. I am not against the principle of writing about the European settlement of Australia from the perspective of the Aborigines. I have simply challenged those who seek to do so from the stand point of their results, their finished product as well as their methodology and purity of purpose. A view of history is a personal matter. However, those who dress and parade their work in the trappings of a scholarly thesis need to remember that they expose themselves to the rigours of the marketplace, to the scrutiny of their peers. Festooning one's work with footnotes, references and bibliographies and then placing a university press imprint on the finished work, is a sure sign you want people to take your work seriously. Therefore, if you lead with your chin and seek the honours and privileges of an academic then you must also bear the responsibilities of the profession.

It has been alleged that there has been a failure of academic quality assurance in Australian universities and issues of bias have also arisen concerning universities. My research as set out above suggests that there appears to have been a failure of academic standards in universities. In fact, it is more than a failure. It could be seen as a breakdown in teaching and supervision or even that of negligence and gross incompetence. It may even be a case of professional misconduct - an intentional act to mislead or fabricate. It is to be hoped that the higher institutions of learning will exercise the legislative powers given to them by parliament to protect their standards and their reputation as centres of excellence.

Epilogue

It is often said that fact is stranger than fiction. Therefore, I cannot end this little saga without informing the reader that in the end everybody lived happily ever after. There can be no greater moment in the history of mankind, than when Ali Baba stood in front of a rock precipice and uttered the words *Open, Sesame!* And to his astonishment, a cave opened up and inside he found riches beyond his wildest imagination. Today the magic phrase is Native Title.

As his Honour Logan J said in *Smith on behalf of the Kullilli People v State of Queensland:*

> 9. The preamble to the *Native Title Act 1993* (Cth) (the Act) recognised, on behalf of all people of Australia, that the Aboriginal peoples of Australia inhabited this country for many years prior to European settlement, and that the Aboriginal peoples had been progressively dispossessed of their lands. It recorded that, by the overwhelming vote of the people of Australia, the Constitution was amended to enable laws such as the Act to be passed, to facilitate the recognition by our shared legal system of the native title rights and

interests in their land. This is an occasion when the Court is to make orders declaring that the groups of Aboriginal persons in the current applications have always been the traditional owners of the land. By the Court's orders, the Australian community collectively recognises that status. It is important to emphasise that the Court's orders do not grant that status. The Court is declaring that it exists and has always existed at least since European settlement.

23. Pastoralists followed the explorers into the region and in 1864 Bulloo Downs was settled, closely followed by Ardoch. Thargomindah was gazetted as a town reserve in 1874 and other smaller townships within the claim area were established soon after. This led to conflict with the indigenous inhabitants of the area. Dr Babidge's Report demonstrates that the Kullilli People endured a period of reprisal and massacre, forced removals and the associated dislocation from country. Many Kullilli People remained on their country working in the pastoral industry which allowed them to continue to exercise and observe their traditional laws and customs (p 51).

24. Dr Babidge identifies the importance of the employment in the pastoral industry which allowed Kullilli People to continue to exercise their traditional activities including the hunting, fishing and observance of traditional law and custom. She says that "there were big camps of Aboriginal people on some stations that enabled the ongoing socialisation of Kullilli people and among them neighbouring groups. Kullilli people lived at Norley Station, Bulloo Downs, Ardock and Mount

Margaret, South Comongin (bordering on the north of Kullilli country), and Nockatunga and others in fairly large camps until the 1940's and 1950's (p 56).[73]

The Federal Court sat in a marquee on an oval at Thargomindah on 2 July 2014 to officially hand down the Native Title determination on a claim first filed in 2009. The court formally recognised the Kullilli people as the traditional owners of 32,000 square kilometres of land in south west Queensland.

---

[73] [2014] FCA 691 (2 July 2014)

Appendix A

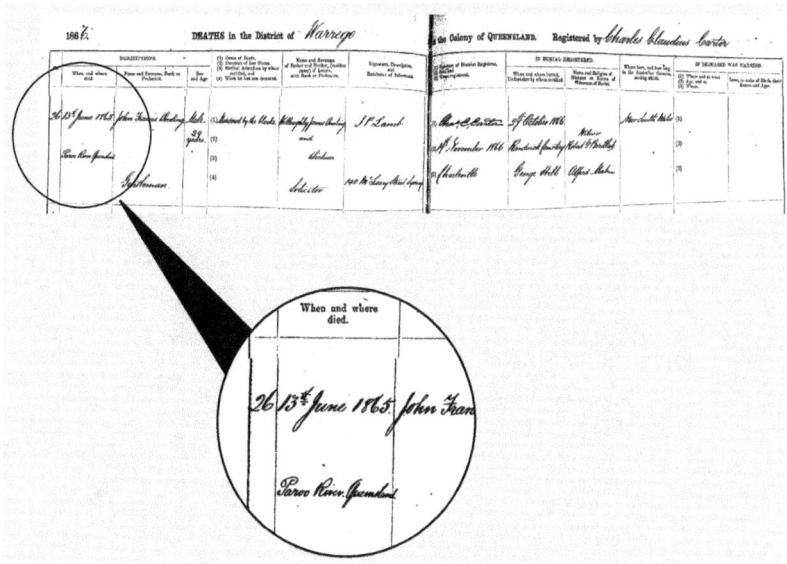

John Francis Dowling's death certificate

Appendix B

Government Advertisements.

PAYMENT FOR SURVEY OF RUNS.

Crown Lands Office,
Brisbane, 8th December, 1865.

THE Licensees and Lessees of the undermentioned Runs are hereby required to pay forthwith into the Treasury the amounts specified in connection with their respective Runs, in accordance with the provisions of the Act 27 Victoria, No. 17.

Attention is called to said clause, which declares that unless payment is made within six months after notification in the *Government Gazette*, all the rights and interests of such defaulters shall be forfeited.

E. W. LAMB,
Chief Commissioner of Crown Lands.

DISTRICT OF WARREGO.

Licensee or Lessee.	Name of Run.	Area in Square Miles.	Amount.
			£ s. d.
A. F. Sullivan	Humeburn North	50	15 0 0
Ditto	Paroo	25	7 10 0
Ditto	Humeburn	50	15 0 0
Ditto	Boobara North	50	15 0 0
Ditto	Boobara	50	15 0 0
Ditto	Humeburn South	50	15 0 0
Ditto	Tilbooroo North	50	15 0 0
Ditto	Boobara South	50	15 0 0
Ditto	Tilbooroo	50	15 0 0
Ditto	Tilbooroo East	50	15 0 0
Ditto	Tilbooroo South	50	15 0 0
G. H. Cox and V. J. Dowling	Upper Eulo Right	50	15 0 0
Ditto	Upper Eulo Left	36	10 16 0
Ditto	Lower Eulo Right	73	21 18 0
Ditto	Lower Eulo Left	50	15 0 0
A. F. Sullivan	Koolyadin	50	15 0 0
G. H. Cox and V. J. Dowling	Kooliatto	50	15 0 0
A. F. Sullivan	Koopa	57	17 2 0
Ditto	Koopa East	50	15 0 0
J. Booker	Koraggarah	50	15 0 0
Ditto	Yungerah	50	15 0 0
Ditto	Lake Colless	75	22 10 0
J. W. Collins, B. C. Hutchinson, and J. Wallis	Owthorpe No. 1	75	22 10 0
Ditto	Owthorpe No. 2	75	22 10 0
Ditto	Owthorpe No. 3	75	22 10 0
Ditto	Owthorpe No. 4	75	22 10 0
Ditto	Owthorpe No. 5	25	7 10 0
Ditto	Owthorpe No. 6	25	7 10 0
Ditto	Owthorpe No. 7	75	22 10 0
Ditto	Owthorpe No. 8	75	22 10 0
Ditto	Owthorpe No. 9	75	22 10 0
Ditto	Owthorpe No. 10	25	7 10 0
J. de V. Lamb, R. K. Sams, and A. J. D. Sams	Quamby	50	15 0 0
G. H. Cox and V. J. Dowling	Wiralla North	50	15 0 0
Ditto	Wiralla	50	15 0 0
J. de V. Lamb, R. K. Sams, and A. J. D. Sams	Norley	50	15 0 0
Ditto	Entally	50	15 0 0
G. H. Cox and V. J. Dowling	Wiralla South	50	15 0 0
J. de V. Lamb, R. K. Sams, and A. J. D. Sams	Huntworth	50	15 0 0
G. Pearson	Thuringowa North	50	15 0 0
J. de V. Lamb, R. K. Sams, and A. J. D. Sams	Lawrenny	50	15 0 0
G. H. Cox and V. J. Dowling	Thuringowa	50	15 0 0
Ditto	Thuringowa South	50	15 0 0
J. de V. Lamb, R. K. Sams, and A. J. D. Sams	Chesthunt	50	15 0 0
Ditto	Chesthunt South	50	15 0 0
G. H. Cox and V. J. Dowling	Kooliatto North	50	15 0 0
R. Russell and C. Bignell	Kargooliah East	50	15 0 0
Ditto	Kargooliah	100	30 0 0
Ditto	Yarranvale	50	15 0 0
Ditto	Buckenby North	50	15 0 0
Ditto	Buckenby West	50	15 0 0
J. Smith	Buckenby	50	15 0 0

Bulloo River Runs
(*Brisbane Courier*, December 14, 1865, p.5.)

Appendix C

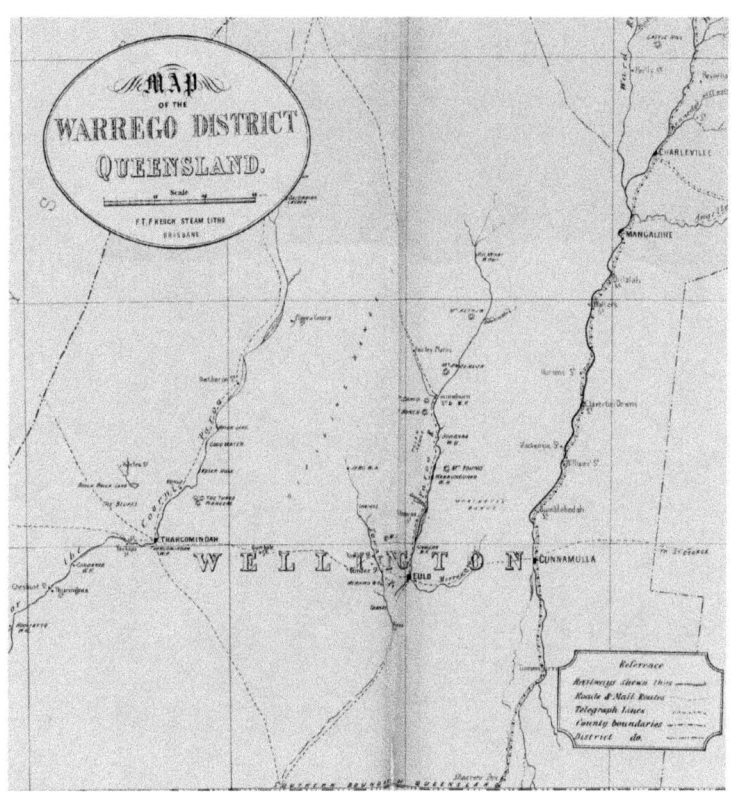

Source: nla.obj 121141766

Appendix D

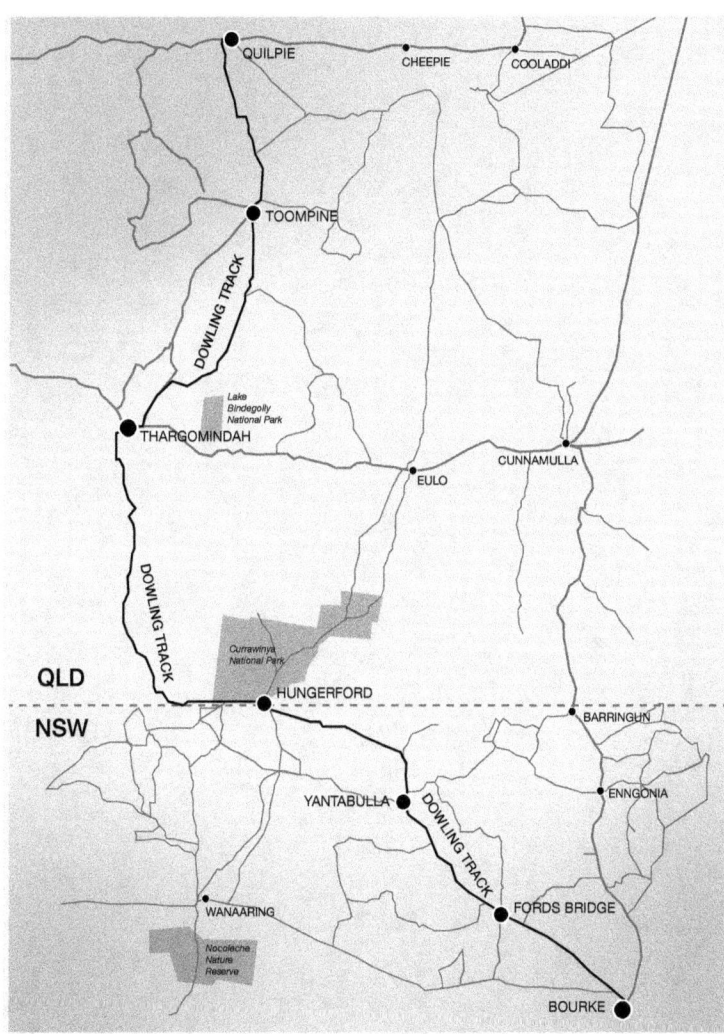

Dowling Track

Appendix E

Letters to the Editor

The Editor of the *Maitland Mercury*.

May I beg you will be good enough to contradict the report of my murder by the blacks to which you have given currency by an extract from some Queensland paper, published in your issue of the 11th ult.

There is not the slightest foundation for the above report. The blacks on the Paroo are the quietest I know in the colonies, and have never interfered with any men in my employ since the formation of the Paroo stations. By your insertion of the above, I shall feel much obliged. I remain, sir, yours faithfully, Vincent Dowling. Warpuelar, Fort Bourke, 1st May, 1864.[74]

Bourke: In reference to the letter sent you by Mr Vincent Dowling, dated Warpuelar and Fort Bourke, May 1st, I have a few words to say. Warpuelar is a station on the Irara, seventy or eighty miles from Bourke, out of the reach of direct traffic, and it is very possible that a letter might

be there till doomsday unless sent in for postage; but from the manner of the dating it is hard to find out

---

[74] *Maitland Mercury and Hunter River General Advertiser,* 12 July 1864, p. 3.

what the writer means to convey. Now, sir, I can inform you that the letter you published and commented on, was written, not at Fort Bourke or Warpuelar, but at Bourke, somewhere about June 23rd, 1864, and which reached you on the 10th of July. You will see that little time was wasted in the transporting; and, in justice to

the inland mails, which have been wrongfully accused of delay, I have mentioned the facts of the case. Of the reported death of Mr Dowling by the blacks, it arose from a shepherd (in the employ of Thom, I think,) named Dowling, falling by the hands of the natives. I have nothing more to say relative to the epistle, only I sincerely trust the writer may never find that he has overestimated the fidelity of the Paroo natives. July 29.[75]

The Editor *Sydney Morning Herald*, **Sydney.**

Through the medium of your valuable journal, I am anxious to contradict certain statements contained in the *Maitland Mercury* of 13th December and 12th January last. The "Bourke Correspondent" of the above-mentioned paper seems gifted with an extraordinary and dangerous mania for grossly exaggerating what he terms OUTRAGES BY THE BLACKS, the locale selected as the scene of these different outrages being

---

[75] *Maitland Mercury and Hunter River General Advertiser*, 9 August 1864, p. 3.

invariably either the Paroo or Warrego Rivers. It would appear from a paragraph in the *Mercury* of the 12th ultimo, that I have been attempting to inculcate a belief in the peacefulness of the blacks which has no foundation. Why the correspondent should accuse me of attempting to induce, such a belief, I am at a loss to imagine; however, I have no hesitation in again stating that the blacks of the Paroo and Lower Warrego are unexceptionably the quietest, most inoffensive, and likely to prove the most useful of any natives I have ever met with. Having but just returned from Bulla, the Paroo, and Charleville, on the Upper Warrego, I am in a position to refute the many startling, and no doubt taking, pieces of information supplied to the *Mercury* by its Bourke Correspondent.

On the Upper Warrego, near the reputed scene of the murder of two of Mr Grenfell's shepherds, there is no such report in circulation. On the Upper Warrego, also, I had, much to my astonishment, the gratification of meeting one of the two men the correspondent had murdered in his blankets. This man, Joseph Nobbs, had been shearing for me, and left to proceed up the Warrego in search of similar employment, when he was stated to have been murdered with his mate. He states there is not the slightest foundation for such a report, and expressed extreme surprise that people should busy themselves in circulating such lies in very forcible language indeed.

The statement of a white man having been murdered at Bulla is utterly false, and without the shadow of a foundation. In reference to another statement made of a man having been MOST BRUTALLY BEATEN by the blacks, near Mr Freers, on the Paroo, I have not heard one syllable, though I have been on the river and close to Mr Freers'.

The circulation by one who should, and must in reality know better, of more vague reports, false and unsubstantial as the above, is injurious, and unnecessarily calculated seriously to cripple and fetter the resources of a young and rising district; therefore, in future, before the medium of the Press is sought to convey to the public mind such startling pieces of information, I should recommend the truthfulness of such report being placed beyond the shadow of a doubt.

In conclusion, I may add that I defy the "Bourke correspondent," or any man, to come forward and prove either of the above-mentioned false and groundless reports. I remain, Sir, Yours faithfully, Vincent Dowling. Warpuelar, Fort Bourke, 28th February.[76]

---

[76] *Sydney Morning Herald,* 28 March 1865, p. 6.

The Editor of the *Maitland Mercury*

My attention has been drawn to certain paragraphs which have from time to time appeared in your paper, purporting to emanate from the pen of your Bourke correspondent; and as many of those paragraphs are not only untrue in themselves, but calculated to seriously injure the character of the district in the minds of those parties to whom our correspondent is personally unknown, I feel it to be a duty to contradict such statements.

The Warrego district, which is, without exception one of the largest and most valuable possessed by Queensland, is not the lawless state your correspondent would evidently lead your readers to believe; and, in proof of my assertion, I challenge him or any other man to come forward and point to any one single instance of a serious crime having been committed upon this river within the past three years, although during that period, and, indeed, up to the present time, we have been, and still are without police protection of any description.

Having made every necessary enquiry into the different outrages said by your correspondent to have been committed by the blacks upon the Paroo and Upper Warrego rivers, I am happy to be in a position to most distinctly and positively deny the truth of such reports. No sheep have been driven away by them, no men have been either beaten or murdered by them. On the contrary, I have no hesitation in asserting that the blacks are, as a body, perfectly inoffensive, quiet, and well disposed; and my experience of them has been such as to induce me to believe that they hereafter are likely to prove most useful, valuable, and trust worthy servants to the residents of the district.

This immunity from crime will, I think, convince every impartial member of the community that in this far-distant portion of the Queensland territory there is greater security both for life and property than in any part of New South Wales; and a statement to the contrary appears to come with a peculiarly bad grace from a resident in the latter colony, where, to judge from the accounts of recent occurrences, the unfortunate inhabitants are liable at any moment to be deprived of the former, and despoiled of the latter without pity, without remorse, by a small number of bloodthirsty scoundrels whom New South Wales, to her shame and disgrace be it said, still permits to rob and murder her children with impunity. I am, sir, yours obediently, Upper Warrego. February 19th, 1865.

[We observe that a similar contradiction has been forwarded to the *Herald*, by Mr Vincent Dowling, of Warpuelar, Fort Bourke, dated 28th February. Mr Dowling enumerates the several statements as to outrages by the blacks which he says have no foundation. We may add that Mr Dowling is not our present correspondent "Upper Warrego." Ed, MM.][77]

Bourke: No rain, and very warm; the river very low, and business even lower. I am sorry to report from the Warrego another death, a bond fide one this time. At this moment there is dying, four miles from Leadanapper, an unfortunate wretch, half eaten by the wild dogs; the police will probably go out and bury the body. This is another victim bordering on Mr Vincent Dowling's "young and rising district," and we warn over again all travellers from approaching that promising region until the rain sets in. All is desolation and aridness for miles; you may proceed without one drop of water from the Culgoa to Dangar's horse-station over one hundred miles; and no water from Bourke to the Warrego. To keep the road, you have fifty to sixty miles without water, and this is Dowling's "rising district." No wonder men sink and perish.

You will see an advertisement in the *Herald* relative to myself, at least it seems such to me. I have not seen it in full. This really clever document bears such undeniable brands of self-gratulation and wounded interest that it is unnecessary for me to say a word; report comes to us hundreds of miles, and, did we guarantee all written about, you would have to forward a very large cheque quarterly;

---

[77] *Maitland Mercury and Hunter River General Advertiser*, 1 April 1865, p. 5.

but this you know, and of course can see the motive of the advertisement. But as Mr Dowling defies "any man" to prove that a man was beaten at Freer's, I accept his challenge, and tell him that although he has not heard one syllable of it a man was cruelly beaten at the above place; and did I feel inclined I could mention two cases in which the advertiser has himself been attacked by the poor peaceful blacks. But enough of this. We are praying for rain in vain. We have a band of bushrangers on the Culgoa. Sergeant Cleary captured some of their horses on the Narran Lake. No news of them lately, Bourke, April 29.[78]

Mr Dowling and the Bourke Correspondent. The Editor of the *Maitland Mercury*.

Having read in a Sydney paper a letter written by Mr Vincent Dowling, accusing your correspondent of untruth and false statement, we beg to say that in no instance has your correspondent said anything but what has been the truth, or what was reported and currently received as truth in this district. Men have been attacked and killed by the blacks, Mr Dowling himself among the former. Men have perished for want of water: N.B., James Dwyer (one of Mr Dowling's men), Kelly, Mason, Richards, and Mr Sullivan's stockman; another is missing; seven or eight men have

---

[78] *Maitland Mercury and Hunter River General Advertiser*, 11 May 1865, p. 3.

been picked up in a dying state. And your correspondent did his duty in warning travellers against coming into this waterless country. This is a perfect desert. You may travel from the head to the foot of the Irara without getting a drink of water, save at Mr Dowling's, and that is not fit to drink. We are only working men; but we read the papers, and know what is the truth and what is the untruth. Begging your pardon for writing you, we remain yours, sir, obliged,

    SAMUEL ROUSE
    THOMAS ENGLISH
    WILLIAM EDYAR
    ANGUS ROSS
    WILLAM B BRIGHT
    THOMAS BRITTON,
Residents of the Warrego River. May 20, 1865.[79]

---

[79] *Maitland Mercury and Hunter River General Advertiser*, 6 June 1865, p. 3.

Appendix F

Edward Owen Hobkirk died at Brisbane, on 30 August 1933, in his 88th year and was privately interred at Ipswich.[80] He was born in Tasmania.[81] So, when he wrote *The Murder of Mr John Dowling. Locality, Bulloo River Queensland*, in 1922, he was already 77 years of age. The manuscript suggests it was written in one sitting from memory. Hobkirk makes the concession in the article that 57 years had lapsed since the events of 1865. Moreover, he left the area in 1888.[82] These circumstances alone would be sufficient to cast a large shadow of doubt over the narrative as to the accuracy and precision of the contents based on the memory of a geriatric and further, that he was hawking the articles round the traps for 10 shillings must suggest it was a quickie for a few bob.

Hobkirk produced over a period of time the following stories:

Early-Day Droving. A Risky Trip by EO Hobkirk, *Daily Mail*, 22 October 1922, p. 19;

Aboriginal Characteristics by EO Hobkirk, *Daily Mail*, 6 January 1923, p. 9;

---

[80] *Courier-Mail*, 31 August 1933, p. 12.
[81] *How I Came To See Chester Win The Melbourne Cup* by EO Hobkirk, *Queenslander*, 30 October 1926, p. 11.
[82] *In A Flood. Personal Experiences In The Far West* by EO Hobkirk, *Queenslander*, 17 July , p. 11.

Impersonating an Aboriginal by EO Hobkirk, *Queenslander*, 12 May 1923, p. 11;

Ladies In The "Never Never" By "Old Jackaroo" Brisbane Courier, 12 July 1924, p. 21;[83]

In A Flood. Personal Experiences In The Far West by EO Hobkirk, *Queenslander,* 17 July 1926, p. 11;

How I Came To See Chester Win The Melbourne Cup by EO Hobkirk, *Queenslander* 30 October 1926, p. 11; and

The Warrego by EO Hobkirk, *Queenslander,* 18 December 1926, p. 11.

The article *Aboriginal Characteristics* appears to incorporate some of the material from *The Murder of Mr John Dowling. Locality Bulloo River Queensland,* I quote as follows:

> Another strange characteristic is that natives seldom will betray their own race. Mr. John Dowling was cruelly murdered by his pet black boy in the Bulloo River district when camped, out together, but this was not proved until many months after. Although the whole, or many of the tribe knew all about it, they would not betray the murderer, so in consequence, sacrificed their own lives.

Now this version is completely different to the version given in *The Murder of Mr John Dowling. Locality, Bulloo River Queensland.*

---

[83] I credit Hobkirk as the author from his tell-tale signature line, "I had known Mr V Dowling since 1865, when I first arrived in the district as a 'jackaroo' at Cheshunt station."

EO Hobkirk's Manuscript

Cover note:

Home Secretary's Office

Brisbane

6/12/1922

An old identity of South West of Queensland called on me and gave me the enclosed. I promised to submit it to you. He said he thought the information was worth 10/-. You may not think so. If you don't, do you mind returning it to me. Wm Gall.[84]

The Murder of Mr John Dowling. Locality, Bulloo River Queensland.

In my long experience among the Western aboriginals in Queensland, I noticed that one of their chief characteristics was that they seldom, if ever, betray their own race. Here is an instance. Mr John Dowling who managed Thouringowa[85] cattle station for his brother, Mr Vincent Dowling[86] was cruelly murdered by his pet blackboy, whom he took with him on an exploring trip to try and discover a practical route to strike the Darling River say somewhere about Manindie (sic Menindee), a small township just formed.

---

[84] William Gall was Under Secretary in the Home Secretary's Department, Brisbane, 30 August 1922.
[85] The correct spelling is Thuringowa. The station eventually became known as Thargomindah.
[86] G. H. Cox and V. J. Dowling held Thuringowa 50 sq miles and Thuringowa south 50 sq miles as at 8 December 1865, see Appendix B. *Brisbane Courier*, 14 December 1865, p. 5.

One morning he made a start on his venture taking with him his pet blackboy (Pimpilly) and that was the last that was seen of him. Many weeks past when Mr Sams[87] of Cheshunt cattle station, where I was employed, received a letter from Mr Vincent Dowling enquiring if he knew anything of his brother Jack. Mr Sams was much surprised at the contents of this, as he (Mr Sams) was under the impression that Mr John Dowling had arrived safely at his destination (the Darling). Mr Sams then came to the conclusion that Dowling had perished or that some serious accident had befallen him and his pilot (the black boy).

Taking his stockman and a black tracker they went in pursuit. At the end of their second day's travelling about 60 miles from Cheshunt they discovered the remains, consisting only of bones, and a scull (sic, skull), which had been dragged about in various directions by the native dogs. There were also the remains of two saddles and a pack saddle, a revolver and a pair of riding boots belonging to Mr Dowling. Not far away from the remains, they discovered the three horses (mudfat)[88]. I believe still with their hobbles on and plenty of water and on good feed. It was rather strange that they did not make their way back to the station. Had they done so, it would have foretold a tale. When Mr Vincent Dowling heard the sad news, he was very math as well as may be expected and cut up.

A short time after he received the sad tidings, he came to Thouringowa Station. I was informed that he (Mr Dowling) had written to the Queensland government authorities concerning the murder and the reply was "to

---

[87] J de V Lamb, RK Sams and AJD Sams held Cheshunt 50 sq miles and Cheshunt South 50 sq miles see Appendix B.
[88] (of animals) very fat.

take what measures he thought best to revenge the murder" as there were no Native Police at that time in the District to see to the matter.

The following procedure was adopted. All the men in the neighbourhood who were available and willing (not including myself) were banded together, armed with revolvers and rifles, set out to revenge the blacks' camp, which was close to the homestead and when doing so there they found belonging of the murdered man consisting of his hat, coat, blankets, tomahawk, sheath knife etc.

Mr V Dowling who could talk the blacks' lingo pretty well asked several of them "who killed white fellah? brother belonging to me." They one and all answered "they knew nothing about the murder." He also enquired, "Where Pimpilly." This they also confessed "that they knew nothing whatever about him." Mr Dowling then said, "If you do not tell me, I will shoot the lot of yous." Still they all remained silent. Mr Dowling and the others, then set to work and put an end to many of them not touching the lubras and young fry. This I know is true as I helped first to burn the bodies and then to bury them. A most unpleasant undertaking but as I was only a jackaroo on Cheshunt station at the time, I had to do what I was told. Later in the day the party went to another camp of blacks about 20 miles down the river and there again shot about the same number.

After the massacre, the whole tribe of blacks left the river frontage and that locality and went miles away out in the ranges and elsewhere. We found it hard to prevent the few that were employed on the stations from doing likewise as they were so scared at what had taken place that we had to lock them up in the hut that was used as a store for a short time. For many months there was not a single black man to be seen for miles around excepting the few already mentioned among these was an elderly man who was deaf and dumb. He gave me and others a demonstration by signs and imitations as to how Mr Dowling was killed. One of these being by holding up one finger evidently meaning that there was only one individual who committed the crime. About 9 months after the above took place the cook and myself were alone at the station (Cheshunt), the manager and the others being absent and not expected to return for some days.

One evening a blackfellow (Tom), a Murry River native who was quite civilised and who could speak good English arrived at Cheshunt from Bulloo Downs station an adjoining cattle station about 40 miles down the river to get mail for that station. He informed me "that about 2 miles away, he had passed a small camp of blacks about 30 in all and that among them he had spied Pimpilly." Who is Pimpilly? I enquired. Why don't you know? he was the boy who was with Mr Dowling and who is supposed to have killed him. Oh! I exclaimed. Then we must collar him, Tom. I at once interviewed the cook (Green) and told him what Tom had told me. I told Tom and Alic (the latter being a Paroo river native, who was also pretty well civilised who was employed at Thouringowa station) to dispense with all their clothing which they did. I gave them each a revolver. Green and myself where (sic) also armed with rifles. I told Tom and Alic to sneak quietly into the camp of blacks locate the culprit and to rush in and grab him. Green and I would keep in the background until he was caught, then we would follow. This was done successfully. The blacks who were all seated then sprang up flourishing their spears and boomerangs and yelling but when they saw two revolvers and two rifles pointed at them, they soon gave in.

The gins were crying, moaning and yelling out baal, baal (meaning no, no, no kill em). The men then settled down and kept quiet. Tom, by this time had fastened the boy's hands behind his back with a saddle strap also put a strap round his neck, attached to it a dog's chain. He was then led by Tom, Alic holding him behind, Green and I walking backwards to keep our eyes on the blacks, kept our rifles ready in case of need etc. The sight of firearms soon quietens aboriginals but never let one walk behind you for that is the time, if opportunity offers, that they will do something desperate. Two mud huts and two tents comprised the homestead at this time. Pimpilly, who appeared to be about 16 years of age, we handcuffed, fastened him about the post of my tent with a dog's chain also a pair of hobbles round his ankles. I then got Tom to ask him in the boy's own language which he (Tom) understood and could speak well to give and explain the full details of the murder. This he did and the following was the blackboys narrative to which I listened must attentively also making notes of same.

On the second night after leaving the station Mr Dowling and he camped without water for themselves or their horses. This annoyed Mr Dowling very much as he quite expected that there would be water as he (blackboy) had said there would. Mr Dowling struck him and called him names for deceiving him regarding the water. After lying down to rest and sleep with his saddle for a pillow (which is the usual custom among Bushmen) Pimpilly seeing that Mr Dowling was sound asleep hit him on the head with a heavy waddy that he had ready. Mr Dowling jumped up grappled with him for a few seconds and then fell down insensible. He then finished off with several hits. His reason for killing him was that he was afraid that Mr Dowling would give him another hiding in the morning as he was doubtful when they would reach water. The following morning, he stripped the body of all its clothing gathered together anything that was of use to him then walked a long way and joined a camp of his tribe in the ranges. The above explanation is proof that the blackboy alone killed Mr John Dowling and by not a number of aboriginals as was stated by the Sydney newspapers at the time of the murder.

The cook and I watched the boy all through the night in turns and kept a strict eye upon him during the day. Towards evening Mr Cameron who was in charge of Thouringowa in the place of the murdered gentleman returned home. I informed him of what had happened during his absence and asked him what he thought was the best thing to do with Pimpilly? He replied "I will take him to the head station to Mr Vincent Dowling." My opinion of this was that it was not a wise plan. However, I gave him up to Mr Cameron. The next day, Mr Cameron took possession of the boy which I was glad of. He fastened his hands together, put him on a quiet horse with Alic (who assisted in capturing him) riding another horse leading the prisoner. It was about 200 hundred miles to Yantabulla station[89] (sheep) where Mr Vincent Dowling lived and the journey occupied 5 or 6 days. Mr Cameron told me he tied him up to a sapling at nights and watched in case he

---

[89] Yantabulla, NSW 2840

should wriggle out of his tackling (blacks are very clever in that way).

Fortunately, Mr V Dowling was absent from there on their arrival, as it would have been very unpleasant for him to see his brother's murderer. He was handed over to Mr Smith who was I believe the overseer. What was done to him I never knew for certain but he was quietly done away with. I presume shoot and buried. Now-a-days, such a case would be very differently dealt with but this happened in 1865, 57 years ago. I knew Mr Vincent Dowling for many years. I often met him but he never alluded to my being instrumental in capturing his brother's murderer. EO Hobkirk

The Murder of John Francis Dowling

Incident	1865 Version	1922 Hobkirk
Deceased Victim	John Dowling	John Dowling
Departure Point	Caiwarroo Paroo	Thouringowa Bulloo
Guide	Waddy Galo	Pimpilly
Reason for travel	Cutting a road	Exploration
Destination	Mount Murchison	Menindee
Duration of travel	Four full days	Not clear/not stated
Search party	Messrs Podmore & Hall	Mr Sams & stockman
Duration of search	Travelled 30 or 40 miles from Paroo	2 days 60 miles from Cheshunt Bulloo
Place of Death	Paroo River Queensland	Bulloo River Queensland
Date of Death	13 June 1865	Not clear/not stated
Environment	Waterless track of country, lost	Good country couldn't locate water
Manner of death	Single blow to head crushing skull	Blow to head struggle then several blows to skull
Reason for death	unknown	To avoid further beatings
Crime scene	Camp site undisturbed	Camp site looted
Perpetrator	unknown	Pimpilly
Horses	Not found	Nearby mudfat plenty of water good feed

Appendix G

Relevant Press Reportage relating to John Dowling's Death

The Maitland Mercury and *Hunter River General Advertiser*, 29 August 1865, p. 3.

The Maitland Mercury and *Hunter River General Advertiser*, 31 August 1865, p. 2.

Empire, 29 August 1865, p. 4.

Empire, 2 September 1865, p. 5.

Empire, 21 September 1865, p. 3.

The Sydney Morning Herald, 1 September 1865, p. 5.

The Sydney Morning Herald, 2 September 1865, p. 5.

The Sydney Morning Herald, 21 September 1865, p. 11.

Illawarra Mercury, 1 September 1865, p. 2.

Sydney Mail, 2 September 1865, p. 2.

Sydney Mail, 2 September 1865, p. 4.

The Newcastle Chronicle and *Hunter River District News*, 2 September 1865, p. 3.

The Armidale Express and *New England General Advertiser*, 2 September 1865, p. 3.

The Brisbane Courier, 2 September 1865, p. 6.

Geelong Advertiser, 4 September 1865, p. 3.

The Herald, 4 September 1865, p. 2.

The Argus, 4 September 1865, p. 5.

The Argus, 5 September 1865, p. 7.

The Age, 5 September 1865, p. 6.

Mount Alexander Mail, 5 September 1865, p. 3.

Clarence and Richmond Examiner and *New England Advertiser*, 5 September 1865, p. 3.

Illawarra Mercury, 5 September 1865, p. 2.

The Toowoomba Chronicle and *Queensland Advertiser*, 7 September 1865, p. 2.

Darling Downs Gazette and *General Advertiser*, 9 September 1865, p. 4.

Burrangong Argus, 9 September 1865, p. 2.

The Australasian, 9 September 1865, p. 11.

Gippsland Times, 9 September 1865, p. 4.

Maryborough Chronicle, Wide Bay and *Burnett Advertiser*, 9 September 1865, p. 2.

Geelong Advertiser, 11 September 1865, p. 3.

Queensland Times, Ipswich Herald and *General Advertiser*, 5 October 1865, p. 3.

Queensland Times, Ipswich Herald and General Advertiser, 17 October 1865, p. 4.

Appendix H

Colonial Frontier Massacres in Central and Eastern Australia 1788-1930

Site Name	Thouringowa Waterhole, Bulloo River, Bullawarra, Thargomindah
Aboriginal Place Name	
Language Group	Kullilla
Colony	QLD
Present State/Territory	QLD
Police District	
Coordinates (imprecise to approx. 250m)	-28.179,143.356,0
Date	Between 1 Jan 1865 and 31 Dec 1865
Attack Time	Daylight
Aboriginal People Killed	300
Aboriginal People Killed Notes	M.W.C
Non-Aboriginal People Killed	0
Non-Aboriginal People Killed Notes	
Attacker Category	Native police
Attacker Details	Native police
Motive	Reprisal
Type Of Motive	Reprisal
Weapons Used	carbines
Notes	
Narrative	Following the killing of Ardoch station owner John Dowling, his brother Vincent led a posse of settlers including EO Hobkirk and set out in revenge and found the Kullila camped on the eastern side of the river and chased them towards the Grey Range, shooting them down as they ran. McKellar says the posse was led by the native police and that 300 were killed.
Sources	Bottoms 2013:63-4; McKellar 1984: 57 (Sources PDF)
Corroboration Rating	**

Version 2.0. The information on this site represents the best evidence available to the research team. It remains subject to change from ongoing feedback, community consultation and research. The research team invites suggestions and corrections.

Stage 2 Research team: Ryan, Lyndall; Pascoe, William; Debenham, Jennifer; Brown, Mark; Smith, Robyn; Price, Daniel; Newley, Jack.

Stage 1 Research team: Ryan, Lyndall; Richards, Jonathan; Debenham, Jennifer; Anders, Robert J; Pascoe, William; Brown, Mark; Price, Daniel.

The information and data on this site may only be re-used in accordance with the *Terms Of Use*. This project was funded by the Australian Research Council Project ID DP 140100399. http://hdl.handle.net/1959.13/1340762.

Bibliography

Bottoms, Timothy, *Conspiracy of Silence Queensland's Frontier Killing Times*, Allen & Unwin, 2013.

Carroll, L., *Through the Looking-Glass*, Raleigh, NC: Hayes Barton Press, 1872.

Copland, Mark et al One hour more daylight: a historical overview of Aboriginal dispossession in southern and southwest Queensland, Editor: Margaret Zucker, Cedar Centre, Toowoomba 2010.

Ewart, HP *Gentleman Squatters, self-made men and soldiers: Masculinities in nineteenth century Australia*, Thesis, University of Adelaide, July 2016.

Hardy, Bobbie Lament for the Barkindji: the vanished tribes of the Darling River region, Rigby, Adelaide 1976.

Maxwell, Charles F Australian Men of Mark 1788 - 1888, Sydney 1888, Vol 1.

McKellar, Hazel Matya-mundu: a history of the Aboriginal people of South West Queensland, edited by Thom Blake, Cunnamulla Australian Native Welfare Association 1984.

Reynolds, Henry *The Other Side of the Frontier*, UNSW Press 2006.

Richards, Jonathan The Secret War, University of Queensland Press, St Lucia, 2017.

Richards, Jonathan *A Question of Necessity: The Native Police in*

Queensland, Thesis, Griffith University, March 2005.

Passionate histories: myth, memory and Indigenous Australia, edited by Frances Peters-Little, Ann Curthoys and John Docker, ANU E Press and Aboriginal History Incorporated 2010.

Warrego and South West Queensland Historical Society, A collection of papers on the history and other subjects to relating to Cunnamulla and district / prepared by members [of] the Warrego and South West Queensland Historical Society. Cunnamulla: The Society; 1969, Vol 1.

Abbreviations

ADB	Australian Dictionary of Biography
DNR	Natural Resources, Mines and Energy, Queensland
ML	Mitchell Library, NSW
MSS	Manuscripts
QSL	Queensland State Library
SMH	Sydney Morning Herald